Short Bike Rides
in Connecticut

"Offers concise directions and maps for [34] different bike rides . . ."
> — *Eastern Mountain Sports Summer Newsletter*

"For anyone with wheels."
> — *Litchfield County* (CT) *Times*

"Detailed directions and maps for two-wheeled tours . . . (a) handy paperback."
> — *Southeastern Connecticut Guide*

Also by Edwin Mullen and Jane Griffith:

*Short Bike Rides on Cape Cod,
Nantucket, and the Vineyard*

Short Bike Rides in Connecticut

Fourth Edition

Edwin Mullen *and* Jane Griffith

An East Woods Book

Chester, Connecticut

All photographs by Edwin Mullen except those on pages xii, 4, 16, 20, 32, 48, 52, 60, 64, 80, 88, 92, 116, and 120 by Henry Hosley; pages 12 and 40 from the State of Connecticut Department of Commerce; page 44 by Hugh and Heather Sadlier; and page 100 by Lisabeth Huck.

Library of Congress Cataloging-in-Publication Data

Mullen, Edwin.
  Short bike rides in Connecticut /Edwin Mullen and Jane Griffith. — 4th ed.
      p.   cm
  "An East Woods book."
  ISBN 0-87106-195-3
  1. Bicycle touring—Connecticut—Guide-books. 2. Connecticut—
  Description and travel—1981- —Guide-books. I. Griffith, Jane, 1934–
  II. Title.
  GV1045.5.C66G75 1992
  796.6'4'09746—dc20   91-39355
                                                                   CIP

Manufactured in the United States of America
Fourth Edition/First Printing

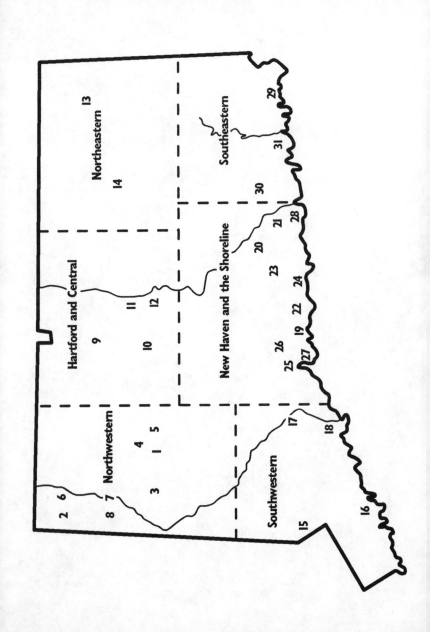

Table of Contents

Northwestern Connecticut

Hartford and Central Connecticut

Northeastern Connecticut

Southwestern Connecticut

New Haven and the Shoreline

Southeastern Connecticut

For the Pros

Introduction

This book combines two unique and pleasurable experiences, riding a bicycle and exploring Connecticut, the exquisite little state the Algonquin Indians called the "place of the long river." That river is the Connecticut, which flows for 407 miles from northern New Hampshire across Massachusetts and Connecticut into Long Island Sound. It would be a short river in the midwest, but in Connecticut, the third smallest state, it's a long river, wide and deep, with relatively little industry or urban sprawl marring its banks.

Connecticut has everything: forests and mountains with whitewater rivers, farms and streams, village greens, lakes, and saltwater beaches, historic houses from the eighteenth century in every town and village and several from the seventeenth. The Guilford ride will lead you to the oldest stone house in America, the beautifully preserved Henry Whitfield house, which dates back to 1639. It's a small museum, and there are many more museums, large and small: Mystic Seaport, with more than 350 years of Connecticut's heritage and tradition on working display in ships and shops of the eighteenth and nineteenth centuries; Hartford's Wadsworth Atheneum; Farmington's Hillstead Museum; the Aldrich in Ridgefield with its fabulous outdoor sculpture; and the traveling museum of the Valley Railroad Company in Essex, which takes you for an hour-long ride on a lovingly restored steam train up to Deep River, where you can embark on an authentic riverboat for a closer look at the Connecticut River and its shores. All of these museums are located along one of our bike rides.

Although it's one of the original thirteen states, Connecticut remains 90 percent woodland, and as you ride through its woodlands or along its shore, you really see everything around you, taking in the full beauty of the sights and sounds and scents of the countryside.

When you stop to pause and reflect with a quiet picnic beside a small lake or stream to rest the bones and improve the spirit, you'll know that the pure joy of bicycles is much more than pedalling.

To get the most out of this book, plan a vacation around it—a four-day weekend or a full week at one of the fine old country inns that grace the Connecticut countryside. They're all in *Recommended Country Inns of New England* by Elizabeth Squier. Choose the area— mountains, flatlands, or shoreline—pick an inn, and, of course, bring your bicycles!

To ensure your enjoyment, take the precautions as outlined in the section on safety and some good equipment. For picnics and swimming, pannier and handlebar bags are indispensable. As to the bike itself, we recommend a good ten- or twelve-speed model of a touring bicycle or, better yet, one of the newer hybrid mountain bikes that have fat but knobless tires and a lighter frame. For the occasional dirt road or a sudden emergency swerve onto a grass or dirt shoulder, these bicycles have it all over the narrow, high-pressure tires of the race-style touring bicycle.

For the racer or long-distance rider we've added a section called "For the Pros."

See you on the road!

Safety

Riding the roads of Connecticut on a bicycle is one of life's rewarding pleasures, but it *can* be dangerous. Some of the rides (i.e., numbers 9. Avon-Simsbury, 11. Hartford, 15. Ridgefield, 17. Shelton-Lake Zoar, and 31. Waterford-New London) include sections that traverse heavily traveled roads, especially on weekdays. If you cannot do these on a weekend, it is advisable to check them out in your car first. Observe all Connecticut state vehicle laws plus those unique to the bicycle: Ride with traffic staying close to the right. Give clear hand signals. Yield to pedestrians. Ride single file. Don't ride on sidewalks in town centers. Check your bike before beginning a trip. Make sure that all nuts are tight and the derailleurs and brakes are working properly. Take a spare tube, a set of plastic tire levers, an air pump, and an adjustable wrench. No matter how long you've been riding, use a checklist before each ride. The one we use appears below.

Checklist

1. Brakes
2. Derailleurs
3. Wheel nuts
4. Tires
5. Lights
6. Reflectors and rear-view mirror
7. Bolt-cutter–proof lock
8. Tool kit
9. Front and rear bags
10. First aid kit
11. Helmet
12. Sunglasses
13. Insect repellent
14. Wash-N-Dry towelettes
15. Picnic ground cloth
16. Food
17. Water bottle
18. Towel and bathing suit
19. Watch
20. Money
21. Reflective vest
22. *Short Bike Rides in Connecticut*

Bantam Lake

Number of miles:	14
Approximate pedalling time:	1½ hours
Terrain:	quite hilly on the east side of the lake, otherwise undemanding
Surface:	good
Things to see:	Point Folly Camp Ground, Bantam Lake, Litchfield Nature Center, Sandy Beach

Bantam Lake, the largest natural lake in Connecticut, encircled by a country road and replete with an uncrowded sandy beach and a 4,000-acre forest, is a jewel of a ride. It begins in Litchfield. Park anywhere along the small Litchfield Green. Mount up and head west on Route 202. In approximately 2¼ miles you will come to North Shore Road on the left, across from the sign, WAMOGO REGIONAL HIGH SCHOOL. Turn left onto North Shore Road to start your loop around Bantam Lake, the largest natural lake in Connecticut. In about a mile you will come to Point Folly Camp Ground, which is a part of the White Memorial Foundation, a 4,000-acre preserve open to the public. (Near the end of the ride you can visit the Nature Center and Museum.)

North Shore Road skirts the end of the lake, winding through an area of modest cottages, swinging to the right, and up a steep, short hill to Route 209. Turn left and in about a mile notice the peninsula of Deer Isle. You will pass several restaurants and places to rent boats. About 4 miles into the ride, you'll arrive at the lake's southern end. Start uphill. At the junction of routes 209 and 109, turn left and continue uphill. Just after reaching the crest of the hill, you'll spot East

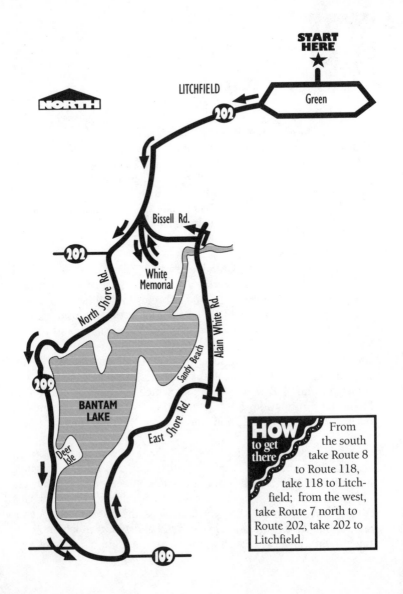

Shore Road on the left; turn here. At the top of your next climb, the road levels off and you'll want to stop to take in the view of the lake. Continue along East Shore Road to Sandy Beach, which is open to the public. Next continue about a mile to where East Shore Road comes to a tee at Alain White Road; turn left. Approximately 9 miles into the ride, turn left onto Bissell Road. You are now on a wide paved road leading through the majestic forest of the 4,000-acre White Memorial Foundation. You will find that hiking trails meander off both sides of this road.

After about 1 mile, turn left into the grounds of the Litchfield Nature Center and Museum. The entrance road is hard-packed dirt.

In ½ mile you'll arrive at the headquarters of the foundation. Here you'll find a large outdoor map of the center's 25 miles of trails; the Nature Center and Museum, with exhibits and restrooms; and many lovely sites for picnicking. The hiking trails are open to bicycles. Fat tires are a distinct advantage! After your ramble through the center, return to Bissell Road. Turn left then immediately right onto Route 202 and head back to Litchfield.

Lakeville—Sharon

Number of miles:	14
Approximate pedalling time:	2 hours
Terrain:	hilly
Surface:	good
Things to see:	Salisbury, Lake Wononscopomuc,
	Lakeville, Hotchkiss School, Mudge
	Pond, Sharon

Lakeville—Sharon is up in Connecticut's mountain country where
the Berkshires, respecting no human boundaries, stride majestically
through New York, Massachusetts, and Connecticut. It's one of four
rides up here: Salisbury—Falls Village, West Cornwall—Furnace
Creek, West Cornwall—Lime Rock, and Lakeville—Sharon. All take
you through the valleys, across the rivers, around the mountains, and
up *some* hills, so it does help to be in good shape when you come up
here. Do come—the scenery is spectacular. Stay at an inn and ride
them all. Try The White Hart Inn in Salisbury, The Inn On Lake
Waramaug, or The Boulders Inn, also on the shore of Lake Waramaug—or camp at Lake Waramaug State Park.

Park your car on Main Street in Lakeville. Head west on Route 44,
which takes you up and down short hills that follow the shape of
Lake Wononscopomuc. In one mile at the top of a hill, you will come
to a fork; bear left. You are now on Indian Mountain Road. Soon you
will have a ½-mile-long downhill. At the bottom of it there is a four-
way stop sign, where Route 112 crosses your street. When you get to
the top of the next ridge, you have a wonderful view of neighboring
valleys and hillsides. Soon there is a mile-long downhill sweep, then
the road levels off, narrows, and comes to a tee almost imperceptibly

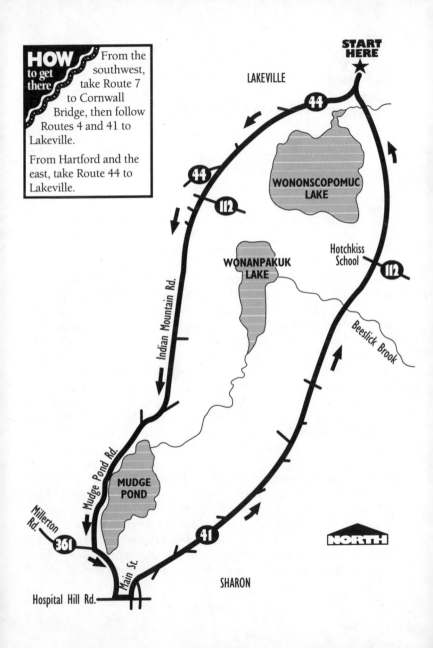

HOW to get there
From the southwest, take Route 7 to Cornwall Bridge, then follow Routes 4 and 41 to Lakeville.

From Hartford and the east, take Route 44 to Lakeville.

START HERE

LAKEVILLE

44

44

112

WONONSCOPOMUC LAKE

WONANPAKUK LAKE

Hotchkiss School

112

Beeslick Brook

Indian Mountain Rd.

Mudge Pond Rd.

MUDGE POND

Millerton Rd.

361

41

NORTH

Main St.

SHARON

Hospital Hill Rd.

at Mudge Road, which comes in from your left and promptly changes its name to Mudge Pond Road. The road makes a sharp right turn and then a sharp left as it nears the pond. After you pass the Sharon Town Beach (residents only, alas), you'll find several beautiful sites for a picnic on the border of the lake.

The route along the pond is about 1½ miles long. Then comes a steep uphill, which takes you out of the valley and yields an expansive view of it. Now the road goes down and comes to a tee at Millerton Road (Route 361). Turn left toward the town of Sharon. Just before the town, the road climbs steeply past a cemetery on the left and then comes to a tee at West Main Street at the Sharon Green. Turn left to explore the village and then turn north on Main Street (Route 41). Route 41 goes uphill out of town. From the crest you can see some of the state's finest scenery. You are skirting a ridge here, going uphill gently at first, then more steeply for ³⁄₁₀ mile, and finally going downhill for ½ mile. This is followed by a long, gradual incline. At the crest take a break to enjoy the panoramic vista that rolls down the valley and across farm after farm to the western horizon—a rare and breathtaking sight. You have earned it. En route again, another long hill takes you to the junction with Route 112. Here ride through the grounds of Hotchkiss School if you like, then continue north on Route 41, enjoying the remaining 2 miles of the ride, which are generally downhill.

Lake Waramaug

Number of miles:	8
Approximate pedalling time:	1¼ hours
Terrain:	flat
Surface:	good
Things to see:	the lake itself, Boulders Inn, The Inn on Lake Waramaug, Hopkins Vineyard Winery, Lake Waramaug State Park

Start the ride at the small but lovely Lake Waramaug State Park. There is ample parking. This park provides camping areas, swimming and picnic grounds, and restrooms, so after you've circuited the lake, plan to spend some time at the park. Mount up and proceed to the right, counterclockwise around the lake. The route is relatively flat and affords fine views of the lake, a large one set down at the base of surrounding hills, which are covered with magnificent foliage, especially in the fall.

After 4 miles of easy riding along the shore of the lake, you will come to the southern end, where there is a commercial boat-launching area, a restaurant, and a beer parlor as well as a town beach. Next is a short uphill stretch on Route 45, leveling off near the Boulders Inn, which offers lodging and dining and has a fine view of the lake. In less than ½ mile you'll come to Lake Road; turn left, leaving Route 45, and continue your circuit. Lake Road is a tiny, narrow road that twists and turns, following the natural contours of the shoreline.

On this stretch you'll come to the Hopkins Inn and Hopkins Vineyard Winery. Turn right and go up a short, steep hill to the winery, which is well worth a stop! The Hopkins family has been farming on this land since 1787. They planted twenty acres of vineyards in 1979,

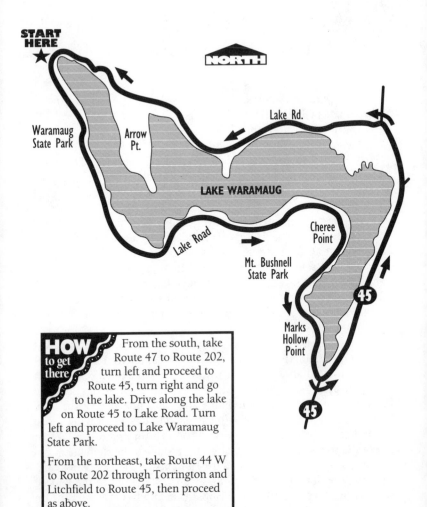

START HERE

NORTH

Lake Rd.

Waramaug State Park

Arrow Pt.

LAKE WARAMAUG

Lake Road

Cheree Point

Mt. Bushnell State Park

45

Marks Hollow Point

45

HOW to get there

From the south, take Route 47 to Route 202, turn left and proceed to Route 45, turn right and go to the lake. Drive along the lake on Route 45 to Lake Road. Turn left and proceed to Lake Waramaug State Park.

From the northeast, take Route 44 W to Route 202 through Torrington and Litchfield to Route 45, then proceed as above.

opened their winery in 1981, and are happy to have you taste their fine whites and reds free of charge.

After your visit, turn right and continue along the hillside for a short distance, until you turn ninety degrees left and rejoin Lake Road. Turn right on Lake Road. Soon you'll see The Inn on Lake Waramaug. This fine old inn, set on a hillside overlooking the lake, has property on the lake front, where there are sailboats and swimming and picnicking for the guests.

As you continue on Lake Road, you will be struck by the fact that long stretches of the shoreline have not been developed. Fields go right down to the water's edge in some places. This is one of the few lakes we have seen that is not entirely taken over by signs saying PRIVATE, KEEP OUT, so riding here is particularly unhurried, unharried, and joyful. Around the next bend you will be able to see the state park. When you come to the entrance, turn left and you are back at your starting place.

We took this ride in October (when the woods were wild with color), and as we rounded the bend into the park, we came upon two cyclist-campers taking a swim after putting up their tent and making camp. As we loaded our bikes for the trip home, we vowed to come back and camp there the following summer.

Litchfield

Number of miles:	4
Approximate pedalling time:	1 hour
Terrain:	flat in town, two hills getting in and out
Surface:	good
Things to see:	Litchfield itself, with its eighteenth-century houses, the country's first law school, Litchfield Historical Museum, the eighteenth-century Congregational church

Litchfield is a short Short Bike Ride, designed to give you a leisurely look at this quintessential New England village of the mid seventeen hundreds. The best way to do it would be to arrive between 10:00 A.M. and 4:00 P.M. on any day except Sunday so you can visit the Litchfield Historical Museum located on the corner of South and East streets before you start out on the ride. It has displays in its four galleries and an outstanding manuscript collection of old Litchfield.

Start at the Litchfield Green. At the east end of the Green, turn right onto South Street (Route 63). Just around the corner there is an entrance into Cobble Court, an old cobblestone courtyard bordered with fascinating shops. Continue down South Street, which is flanked on both sides by eighteenth-century homes, one of which housed the first law school in America, started in 1775 by Tapping Reeves, whose brother-in-law, Aaron Burr, was his first pupil. It matriculated more than one thousand students before it closed in 1833.

When you get to the intersection of South Street and Old South Street, notice the Ethan Allen House, built in 1736. This house is be-

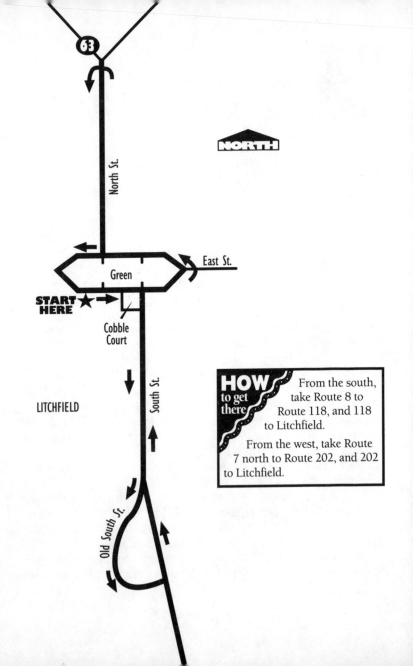

63

NORTH

North St.

Green

East St.

START HERE ★

Cobble Court

South St.

LITCHFIELD

Old South St.

HOW to get there

From the south, take Route 8 to Route 118, and 118 to Litchfield.

From the west, take Route 7 north to Route 202, and 202 to Litchfield.

lieved to have been the birthplace of the Revolutionary War hero. Bear right and follow Old South Street for approximately 1³⁄₁₀ miles as it loops back to South Street, where you turn left and go uphill back to the Green. On South Street the sidewalk is broad and passes close to the lovely old houses; it's a good place to ride if there is not too much pedestrian traffic. Watch for the Oliver Wolcott, Sr., House (Wolcott, governor of Connecticut, was a signer of the Declaration of Independence). Turn right when you arrive at the Green, circle around the end of the Green and proceed to the intersection with North Street (Route 63 north). There are stately homes on both sides of North Street, including, on the west side, Sheldon's Tavern where George Washington once slept. Go up one side of North Street and down the other, using the Alexander Catlin House (1778) at the Y as the turn-around point. Return to the Green.

Litchfield County

Number of miles:	12
Approximate pedalling time:	2 hours
Terrain:	definitely hilly
Surface:	mostly good, some bad spots
Things to see:	superb Connecticut farmland and woods, fine houses of Litchfield

If you would like a leisurely, French-countryside kind of a picnic, under a tall shady tree with cows lowing on the other side of a New England stone wall, load your pannier bags with all the fixings and take this ride, starting from the Litchfield Green. Turn left onto Route 202 and ride approximately 1 mile to the point where Brush Hill Road angles off at forty-five degrees to your right. Turn right onto Brush Hill Road, and in about ½ mile you will pass a long, low stone wall on the left. This was once the site of the Kilravock Inn. In the original edition of our book the Litchfield rides started from this inn. Alas, the beautiful inn burned to the ground several years ago and is no more.

After 1½ miles of uphill riding through the woods, Brush Hill becomes Maple Street at a stop sign. Continue on Maple Street, passing Litwin Road on the left. Soon you will come to the intersection of Maple and Milton Road. Turn right onto Milton, which meanders, going uphill and down (as do all these roads). You will pass the Stony Brook Golf Course. Two miles after turning onto Milton, you will come to Osborn Road on your left. Turn up Osborn for a short, steep push. Within ½ mile Osborn merges with Beach Street.

As you join Beach Street, you will bear slightly left and in approximately 1 mile you'll come to the lovely spot where your authors pic-

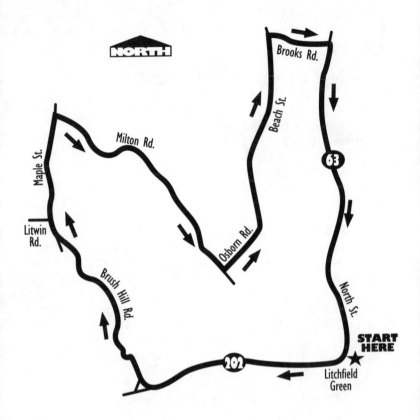

NORTH

Brooks Rd.

Beach St.

Milton Rd.

Maple St.

Litwin Rd.

Osborn Rd.

63

Brush Hill Rd.

North St.

START HERE

202

Litchfield Green

HOW to get there From the south, take Route 8 to Route 118, and 118 to Litchfield.

From the west, take Route 7 north to Route 202, and 202 to Litchfield.

nicked when creating the ride. Our lunch under a stately tree was accompanied by the lowing of a clutch of mildly curious cows on the other side of the fence.

Back on the road, you'll enjoy the views occasionally revealed through the trees and the large country homes you will pass. Two miles from the intersection of Osborn and Beach, you come to Brooks Road; turn right. The street sign here may be twisted, showing the street names reversed, but 'tis not so. You *have* been on Beach Street and are turning onto Brooks Road, which immediately goes downhill and then abruptly uphill before descending again to Route 63. Brooks Road forms a tee with Route 63. Turn right. There is a stop sign for you; be cautious.

You are about 3 miles from Litchfield, and you face a couple of arduous uphill climbs, barely relieved by brief downhills. In Litchfield, Route 63, also called Goshen Road, becomes North Street. This street is flanked by some of America's architectural treasures. From the size and immaculate condition of all these eighteenth- and nineteenth-century homes it appears that only the houses of the wealthy were worth preserving over such a long period of time, creating a Litchfield of today very different from what it was 200 years ago.

Salisbury—Falls Village

Number of miles:	19
Approximate pedalling time:	2½ hours
Terrain:	varied, some tough hills, some rolling country, some flat stretches
Surface:	generally good
Things to see:	Salisbury and Falls Village, Great Falls, Lime Rock Park, Berkshire foothills, Salmon Creek Valley

This is mountain country, Connecticut style. It isn't the Rockies or the Alps, but it's beautiful—as you will soon see. Park anywhere on Main Street and head north on Route 44 east. In a half mile you'll go uphill and crest at the entrance to Salisbury School. Parts of the climb are very steep but are followed by a mile-long downhill with a view of the Berkshires. Half a mile from the bottom you'll cross the Housatonic River and make a right turn onto Route 126 heading for Falls Village. In 1½ miles you'll cross a single railroad track and come to the junction with Sand Road, which comes in from the left. Bear right and cross the bridge over the Hollenbeck River. Off the road, on the left, is a small white sign: STATE OWNED PROPERTY—HUNTING PERMITTED. So, this stretch of river belongs to you and me and it's a lovely spot for a picnic—and, if you're so inclined, a dip in an old-fashioned swimming hole. Your authors did both one Fourth of July, and nary a car went by.

Continue on 126 (here called Point of Rocks Road) and when it turns left, go straight on Point of Rocks Road downhill to a Y fork. Bear right, under the railroad, ninety degrees right, past the hydroelectric power plant and left across the one-lane bridge. The tiny

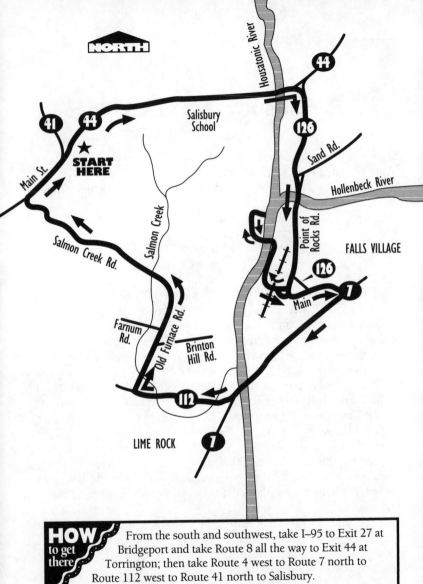

NORTH

Housatonic River

44

41

44

Salisbury School

126

Sand Rd.

Main St.

★ START HERE

Hollenbeck River

Salmon Creek Rd.

Salmon Creek

126

Point of Rocks Rd.

FALLS VILLAGE

7

Main

Farnum Rd.

Old Furnace Rd.

Brinton Hill Rd.

112

7

LIME ROCK

HOW to get there

From the south and southwest, take I–95 to Exit 27 at Bridgeport and take Route 8 all the way to Exit 44 at Torrington; then take Route 4 west to Route 7 north to Route 112 west to Route 41 north to Salisbury.

From the New Haven area, take I–91 north to Exit 17, I–691 west to I–84 west to Route 8 at Waterbury, then 8 north.

riverside park on the left has restrooms and an ominous sign, WHEN HORN SOUNDS WATER WILL BE RISING! It's a lovely spot to rest and pic-nic—just be ready to move if the horn sounds! It means the power plant has stopped diverting the river water up at the small dam, and the river will be going over the falls again. To see the falls, go back to-ward the bridge but don't go over it; turn left and then right. In less than ½ mile you'll see the dam and either a first-class waterfall or a trickle, depending on whether the power plant is operating or not.

Retrace your route over the bridge, back under the railroad, and up and right at the Y fork to Main Street, where you turn left. On a plaque on the Green you'll learn that *Housatonic* means "place be-yond the mountains." In Falls Village note the stately National Iron Bank and across from it an old church-cum bookstore full of old and rare books. Go on in. You are sure to come out with at least one book.

When Main Street rejoins Route 126, take 126 to Route 7. Turn right on Route 7 for Lime Rock 3 miles away. When you come to the junction with Route 112, go right on 112 to Lime Rock, which boasts that it is "the Road Racing Center of the East."

After you go over the second, larger bridge over Salmon Creek, turn right at the first road, Furnace Road. After a short and abrupt uphill on this one lane road, you'll come to a small, diamond-shaped Y; bear right on what is now Old Furnace Road, which takes you down into Salmon Creek Valley. In about ½ mile the road forks; bear right onto Salmon Kill Road (Did you know that *kill* means creek?) Salmon Kill Road may not be marked here, so be sure you pass Brin-ton Hill Road, which goes up to your right. The road follows the con-tours of the mountains, the tallest of which, Raccoon Hill (1100 ft.), is ahead and to your right. About ½ mile past the Farnum Road junc-tion, the road will turn sharply left crossing the valley floor. For the next 1½ miles you'll wind through lovely country on the west side of the valley before you come to a tee at Salisbury's Main Street. Turn right. At the corner of Washinee Street enjoy the delicious spring water of the public fountain. Continue up Main Street to your start-ing place.

West Cornwall— Furnace Creek

Number of miles:	12
Approximate pedalling time:	1½ hours
Terrain:	rolling on the west side of the Housatonic, hilly on the east
Surface:	good
Things to see:	an authentic covered bridge, the Housatonic River, Housatonic Meadows State Park, Furnace Creek, the village of West Cornwall

West Cornwall serves as the starting-off place for two beautiful rides, this one and West Cornwall—Lime Rock. Both come and go through one of the last of the original covered bridges in Connecticut. This one was designed by Ithiel Town and has been in continuous use since 1837.

Park anywhere on West Cornwall's hilly main street. You should explore this tiny village, perched on the side of the restless, beautiful Housatonic River, either before or after your ride. There are interesting shops, including the Tollhouse. The Fresh Fields Restaurant and Gift Shop serves good food—indoors and out. In clear weather you can dine on the restaurant's deck, which is built out over a rocky brook and waterfall. A stop here is a great reward, especially after your ride. Another plus on this ride is that there are numerous lovely places to picnic, either on the banks of the Housatonic or along Furnace Creek.

Start the ride by crossing the river over the covered bridge. Turn left on the other side and go south on Route 7 along the river's edge. You may see canoeists or swimmers tubing where the river is swift

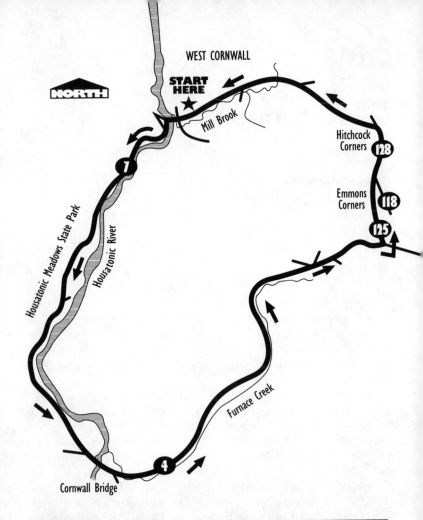

WEST CORNWALL

NORTH

★ START HERE

Mill Brook

Hitchcock Corners **128**

Emmons Corners **118**

125

Housatonic Meadows State Park

Housatonic River

7

Furnace Creek

4

Cornwall Bridge

HOW to get there

From the north or south, take I–91 to the I–691 exit at Meriden. Take I–691 west to I–84 west to Route 8 north to Torrington. Then take Route 4 west to the junction of Routes 4, 43, and 128. Take 128 north to West Cornwall.

From the southeast, take Route 8 north from Bridgeport.

but not overly dangerous. You will see very few houses on the ride as your road dips and winds gently up and down hill, following the contour of the Housatonic, accompanying it on its long journey to Long Island Sound. It's a magical sight.

In 2½ miles you will come to a campsite that is one of the most inviting we've seen: Housatonic Meadows Campground. One mile further brings you to the park's adjoining picnic grounds for noncampers. In about 4 miles you will come to the junction where Route 4 joins Route 7. Bear left and cross the river at the Cornwall Bridge. Stop on the bridge for a while to take in the scene: river, rocks, clouds above, shades of green, houses tucked into hills.

There is a fork just over the river. Bear left on Route 4 where you must master a steep hill. Route 4 borders Furnace Creek, and there are many superb picnic sites just off the road. We stopped and had lunch about ½ mile from the fork at a lovely spot with a creek right under our feet, just *before* a turnout on the right (with a picnic table in it).

About 8 miles into the ride, you will come to the junction of Routes 4 and 125; turn left and go up a steep hill toward West Cornwall through woods and forest. Soon Route 128 joins 125 at an oblique angle from the right. About ½ mile from town you will start a long winding descent into the village—a great way to end the ride!

West Cornwall— Lime Rock

Number of miles:	16
Approximate pedalling time:	2 hours
Terrain:	definitely hilly, with a long incline and some good downhills
Surface:	good
Things to see:	the hillside village of West Cornwall, the covered bridge, Lime Rock Raceway, the wildlife sanctuary, the splendor of northwest Connecticut's mountains and forests

This ride was suggested by Alan Momeyer and Janet Markoff of New York, who discovered it in the summer of 1983 while using this book as their "main guide for a wonderful four-day weekend of biking."

After arriving in West Cornwall, park your vehicle anywhere along the village's inclined main street—the best place is probably the post office lot, only ⅕ mile from the river. You've got 16 miles of delightful, soul-satisfying bicycle riding to look forward to, so I recommend exploring the little village when you get back.

Start by crossing over the river on the old, one-lane covered bridge, turning right on the other side to go north on Route 7. The Housatonic is within earshot on your right, and silent forests tower up on your left. For 4 miles your road rolls up and down, changing every ⅕ mile! At the 4-mile point, you'll come to the junction of Route 112 with 7 north, which curves right. You should bear left onto 112.

For 2 miles this road will prove wider, flatter, and smoother than the forest roller coaster you've just left, but it provides a pleasant change with its lovely picture-postcard homes from the late nine-

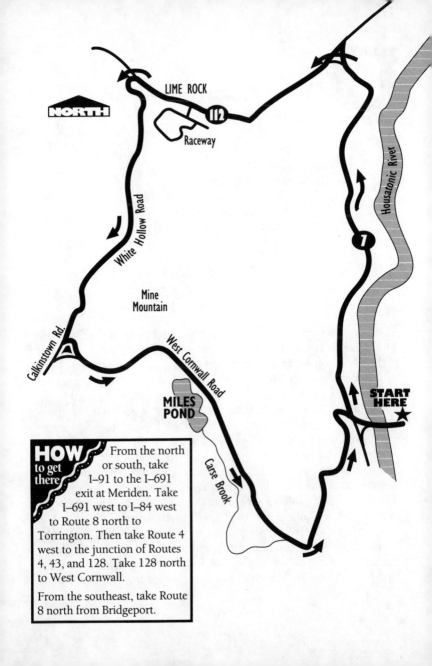

NORTH

LIME ROCK

112

Raceway

Housatonic River

White Hollow Road

Mine
Mountain

Calkinstown Rd.

1

West Cornwall Road

MILES
POND

START
HERE

Carse Brook

HOW to get there — From the north or south, take I–91 to the I–691 exit at Meriden. Take I–691 west to I–84 west to Route 8 north to Torrington. Then take Route 4 west to the junction of Routes 4, 43, and 128. Take 128 north to West Cornwall.

From the southeast, take Route 8 north from Bridgeport.

teenth century. Within 1¼ miles at the crest of a hill, Lime Rock Raceway comes into view over on the left. As Alan and Janet put it, the raceway "might be a fun pit stop." About ¾ mile further on, 2 miles from Route 7, you'll cross over a bridge and immediately make a hairpin left turn downhill onto White Hollow Road, which then quickly twists to the right, still going downhill. For the next 4½ miles you'll be on a roller coaster once again, passing beautiful early twentieth-century homes with sculpted farmland in the background. Then you'll come to a T intersection with a little grassy island separating two country roads, West Cornwall Road, which you will take to the left, and Calkinstown Road to the right (White Hollow Road, having done its work, ends its life here).

Once you have turned left onto West Cornwall Road, get ready! You're about to enter a primeval swamp and forest preserve, 5 miles of wildlife sanctuary, with "all plants and animals protected by State and Federal Law and by the National Audubon Society." The preserve lies within a valley between the mountains of the Housatonic State Forest. Mine Mountain is the one you can see rising up behind the first swamp on the left. You will probably be the only human being on the road. Bring binoculars, ride slowly, and absorb the mysteries of the wildlife.

In about 1½ miles, Miles Pond will appear on the right, then Carse Brook, and then suddenly a startling sight appears—a magnificent, two-story stone house bearing an air of antiquity about it, quiet, out of place, as though materialized by Prospero's magic from seventeenth-century England. It's just off the road; next to it is a stone swimming pool, guarded by two large bronze statues, and then you'll see a sign: MILES WILDLIFE SANCTUARY.

After you enter the land of private property once again, in about 1 mile the road heads sharply downhill to the left, zigzags steeply down ninety degrees to the left, cuts a hard right, levels off, and then goes steeply down and to the right again, ending abruptly at a tee with Route 7. You'll find yourself just across from the covered bridge to West Cornwall!

9

Avon—Simsbury

Number of miles: 20
Approximate pedalling time: 2 hours
Terrain: mostly gentle, one notably long hill
Surface: fair
Things to see: Avon, Avon Park, Avon Old Farms School, Simsbury, Massacoh Plantation, Ethel Walker School, Stratton Brook State Park

Avon—Simsbury has much to offer, from the sight of a small seventeenth-century English village that turns out to be a boys' school to what must be the only secret bike path in Connecticut, known only to those who live near it and you, dear reader.

The best place to start is from the parking lot at the Old Avon Village Shopping Center, which is located a short distance back from the southeast corner of the intersection of Routes 44 and 202, where 44 goes straight and 202 turns and goes north.

Come out of the parking lot, turn left using the sidewalk (walking your bike), go the short distance to the intersection of 44 and 202, and turn left onto Old Farms Road. You're on your way!

In about 2 miles you'll arrive at the entrance to Avon Old Farms School, which is marked by an enormous brick tower. Pass the tower and turn left into the driveway and ride up to the main building. This boys' school is built in the style of an Elizabethan village. It is an enchanting sight. Leave by the exit driveway, turn right at the gate, and ride the few yards to Scoville Road. Turn left onto Scoville; in ½ mile, turn right onto Burnham Road. When Burnham forms a tee with West Avon Road (Route 167), turn right.

Cross Route 44 and head toward Simsbury on Route 167 (now

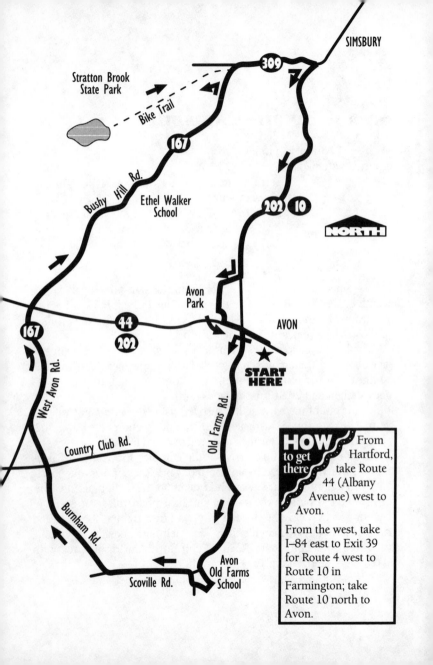

SIMSBURY

Stratton Brook
State Park

Bike Trail

309

167

Bushy Hill Rd.

Ethel Walker
School

202 **10**

NORTH

Avon
Park

AVON

167

44
202

West Avon Rd.

★ **START HERE**

Country Club Rd.

Old Farms Rd.

Burnham Rd.

Scoville Rd.

Avon
Old Farms
School

HOW to get there From Hartford, take Route 44 (Albany Avenue) west to Avon.

From the west, take I–84 east to Exit 39 for Route 4 west to Route 10 in Farmington; take Route 10 north to Avon.

called Bushy Hill Road). There is a long incline on this stretch. You'll pass the Ethel Walker School, cross Stratton Brook Road, and, in about a mile, come to the T intersection with Route 309. Within a few feet of this intersection, on the left side of Route 167, there is a small opening in the trees. This is the beginning of a hidden bike path, running for a mile straight to Stratton Brook Park. Cross the road and get on it. The transition is swift and startling—from asphalt, traffic, and noise to the hush of a leafy wonderland. The trail of hard-packed earth ends at the lake in the center of the park. Here you may swim, hike, and picnic. The restrooms and dressing cubicles across the pond are closed after Labor Day. But there's no need to hide behind a tree if you come later on. The park department has supplied two outhouses for those who like to ride in the fall or winter.

Return to Route 167 on the bike trail. As soon as you're back on 167, turn right at the T with 309, heading towards Simsbury. At the stoplight marking the intersection of Routes 309 and 202, you have a choice: turn right and head toward Avon, 4 miles away, or take a left and detour through the town of Simsbury and visit the Massacoh Plantation, an interesting museum on Simsbury's main street. After returning to the intersection of Routes 309 and 202, proceed south on 202. A sidewalk along this stretch of highway should be used since the road is narrow and heavily traveled. This section of Route 202 runs parallel to the Farmington River, hidden off to your left, flowing at the foot of a high ridge, which comes into a magnificent view about a mile down 202. The tall tower, rising 165 feet above the ridge, was once the summer home of the Heublein family.

Back in Avon, turn right on Fisher Drive, which is just before Sperry Park on the left side of Route 202, and go past the first road on your left. Take the next one on the left, Ensign Drive, and you'll soon see the renovated factory complex now harboring Avon Park and the Farmington Arts Center. The town offices are also here—complete with restrooms. There are exhibits in the gallery of the Arts Center and artists' studios in the adjoining brownstones. (This delightful complex used to be a fuse factory!) Go out the park's exit to Route 44, turn left, and return to the Old Avon Village Shopping Center 1½ blocks away.

Farmington

Number of miles:	14½
Approximate pedalling time:	2 hours
Terrain:	varied, some short steep hills
Surface:	good
Things to see:	Batterson Park, Stanley-Whitman House, Miss Porter's School, Hill-Stead Museum, the Grist Mill

Farmington is one of those Connecticut towns and villages that were founded before the American Revolution and bear the label "quaint" but are indeed far more than that tainted word implies. Farmington, like many others, is inhabited by people who care about the part their town played in American history and in maintaining the buildings and traditions from the past, but they also live very much in the present—all of which makes their town a fascinating place to explore.

Batterson Park is to the east of I–84, so if you come off I–84 from the north, turn left and cross over 84 on Fieneman Road and then turn left onto Batterson Park Road. From the south go right and then left. The park is open to the public on weekends and holidays only from 9:00 A.M. to 8:00 P.M., so if you'd like to picnic or swim after visiting the town it would be best to come on the weekend. Start out by taking Batterson Park Road about a mile back to the intersection with Fieneman Road (the first traffic light). Turn right on Fieneman. Within ½ mile you'll come to the intersection of Fieneman, Colt Highway, and Birdseye. Cross Colt Highway at a forty-five-degree angle onto Birdseye, then turn left onto Mountain Road, the first left.

After a mile turn left at the stop sign onto Reservoir Road, keeping a sharp eye out for traffic coming up the road from your right. In

37

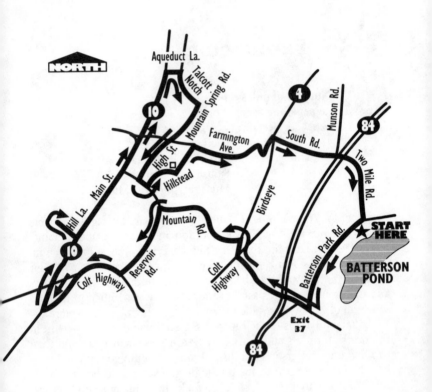

HOW to get there From the north, take Route 84 to Exit 37 (Fieneman Road), follow the signs to Batterson Park.

From the south, take I–91 to the Meriden exit for I–691 west. Take 691 west to I–84 and 84 north to Exit 37 to Batterson Park.

about a mile turn right onto Colt Highway. As you go down this hill, bear diagonally left, following the signs to Route 10, which is at the bottom of the hill. Turn right on 10. Within a mile you'll be in the beautiful town of Farmington. Take a side trip to the Grist Mill by turning left on Mill Lane (across from the Congregational church) and going down to the Farmington River. In the mill there's a bookstore, which has carried this book for many years. Back on Main Street (Route 10), ride by the Congregational church and the buildings of Miss Porter's School.

Cross Route 4 (Farmington Avenue) at the traffic light and continue on Route 10 north about 2 miles, past the golf course, to Aqueduct Lane. Turn right, and go up this short but steep hill to a tee intersection with Talcott Notch Road, where you turn right. At Mountain Spring Road, turn right again, and within another 1½ miles you'll be back at Farmington Avenue. Turn right onto Farmington, go down a short, steep hill to High Street, where you turn left at the caution light, exercising extreme caution.

Midway up High Street you'll see the Stanley-Whitman House (1660). It's open to the public on Sundays only. There is a small entrance fee.

When you reach Mountain Road (a tee intersection), turn left and go a short distance uphill to the entrance driveway to the Hill-Stead Museum. Turn left and ride through the grounds to the Stanford White–designed house. Hill-Stead is an unusual museum in that the owners stipulated that it was to remain exactly as it had been when they lived in it, with their beautiful paintings and sculpture by Manet, Monet, Degas, and other French Impressionists in their original settings. It is open May through October, noon to 5:00 P.M. and November through April, noon to 4:00 P.M. A moderate admission fee is charged.

When you are ready, continue the ride by going around the back of the house and down through the property to Farmington Avenue (Route 4). Turn right. In ½ mile, follow Route 4 east as it circles ninety degrees left, crossing Farmington Avenue, then turn right onto South Road. In a mile, Munson Road will merge into South Road from the left. Go over the highway and continue for about ½ mile on what is now called Two Mile Road to Batterson Park.

Hartford

Number of miles: 11
Approximate pedalling time: 1½
Terrain: generally rolling, three hills
Surface: fair to good; watch for road work in progress
Things to see: Constitution Plaza, Old State House, Wadsworth Atheneum, Bushnell Plaza and Park, State Capitol, State Museum, Mark Twain House, Harriet Beecher Stowe House, Elizabeth Park, Governor's Mansion, Hartford Civic Center

There's much to see in Hartford, but it's best to make this a weekend ride. Hartford traffic during the week is too much to cope with, and the streets become user-*un*friendly.

Park your car near award-winning Constitution Plaza on Columbus Boulevard. Start your ride on State Street in front of Broadcast House. Turn left onto Prospect Street, passing in front of the Old State House on Thomas Hooker Square. Go 2 blocks to Atheneum Square North; turn right. You will pass the Travelers' Insurance Co., the Avery Memorial, and the Wadsworth Atheneum, a nationally recognized fine arts museum. Cross Main Street, passing Bushnell Plaza. Go downhill to Bushnell Park. Ride into the park and cross it on the diagonal crossway. You will come out of the park at the corner of Elm and Trinity streets; turn left. The stone arch on the right is a Civil War memorial.

At the top of the hill turn right and circle around the Capitol,

NORTH

Elizabeth Park

Prospect St.

Albany St.

Whitney

Scarborough St.

Fern

Sherman St.

Seminary

Woodland St.

Collins St.

Farmington Ave.

Asylum St.

84

Garden St.

Myrtle St.

State Capitol

Park

Park

Church St.

Atheneum Sq. No.

State St.

Constitution Plaza

Main St.

Talcott St.

Prospect St.

Columbus Blvd.

★
START HERE

HOW to get there
Take the State Street Exit 31 from I–91 if you are coming from the north or south, or the State Street exit from I–84 or Route 15 if you are coming from east or west.

passing the State Museum on the left. You can see the Armory below the Capitol as you make the circle. When you come around to the side of the Capitol overlooking the city, take the paved pathway going down the hill, bearing left on the intersecting path to Asylum Street. Turn left on Asylum, and when it forks, bear left on Farmington. On this street you will pass some of the insurance companies for which Hartford is famous, as well as the city's new cathedral.

After 3 miles on Farmington, you will come to Nook Farm. On this tract stand the houses of two of America's most celebrated writers, Mark Twain and Harriet Beecher Stowe. The houses are open to the public.

After you've seen one or both, turn right in a few blocks onto Sherman Street, which curves left in the middle of the Hartford Seminary and becomes Fern Street. Go up Fern to Whitney. Turn right onto Whitney and then left into Elizabeth Park at the corner of Whitney and Asylum. Circle through the lower half of the park, then cross Prospect and enter the upper half of the park. Ride around the superb Rose Garden back to Asylum Avenue; turn right. At the corner of Prospect and Asylum, where the Governor's Mansion is located, turn left. A long hill leads you past the mansion to Albany Street. Turn right and ride downhill to Scarborough Street. Turn right onto Scarborough and go to Asylum and turn left.

Proceed to Woodland Street; turn left here (at the St. Francis Hospital and Medical Center), then turn right on Collins Street. Ride about seven blocks on Collins and then turn right onto Garden Street. Go up a short, steep hill and turn left onto Myrtle. Go downhill for one block, bearing right (Myrtle becomes Church Street here), then left under the railroad station. You will pass the mammoth Hartford Civic Center. Church Street forms a tee with Main Street in front of the well-known G. Fox and Co. store. Turn left; go a scant block to Talcott Street. Turn right onto Talcott and ride down to Columbus Boulevard and your car.

Wethersfield

Number of miles:	11½
Approximate pedalling time:	1½ hours
Terrain:	varied, some steep hills
Surface:	generally good, some poor spots
Things to see:	Buttolph-Williams House, Silas Deane House, Joseph Webb House, Isaac Stevens House, Old Academy Museum, Comstock-Ferre Co., Wethersfield Cove, Millwoods Park

Wethersfield is one of the towns where history was made, and there's much to see. Start the ride on Main Street across from the Comstock-Ferre Co., Connecticut's oldest seed company and a good place to browse. Ride north on Main Street past many handsome houses to the shore of Wethersfield Cove and Common. This is a busy boating scene in the summer. Return down Main Street and turn left on Marsh Street. Ride past the cemetery and turn right on Broad Street. The marvelous Buttolph-Williams House (1692) stands silently on the corner. This house contains an excellent collection of period pieces, including an extensively furnished kitchen. Proceed on Broad Street to the Wethersfield Green. Bear left and ride down the left side of the Green. At the end turn right and come back up the right side as far as Garden Street. Turn left on Garden and go to Main. Turn right. Pass the Old Academy Museum. In another block you will come to a trio of stately houses. The Silas Deane House (1766) is the first of these. General Washington planned the capture of Fort Ticonderoga in this elegant house. The Joseph Webb House (1752) was also graced by the presence of General Washington, for here he met with

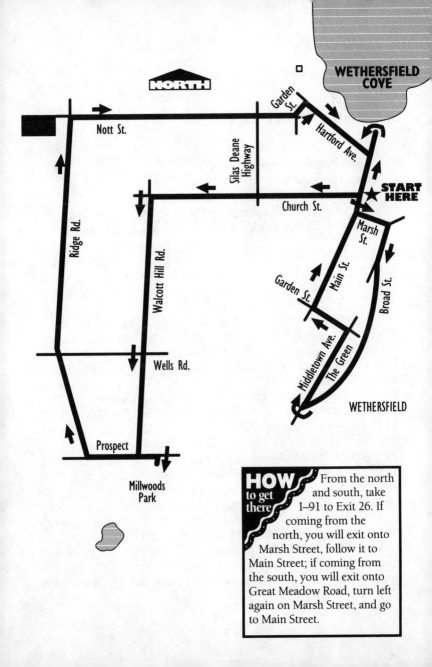

NORTH

WETHERSFIELD COVE

Garden St.

Nott St.

Hartford Ave.

Silas Deane Highway

START HERE

Ridge Rd.

Church St.

Marsh St.

Walcott Hill Rd.

Garden St.

Main St.

Broad St.

Middletown Ave.

The Green

WETHERSFIELD

Wells Rd.

Prospect

Millwoods Park

HOW to get there — From the north and south, take I–91 to Exit 26. If coming from the north, you will exit onto Marsh Street, follow it to Main Street; if coming from the south, you will exit onto Great Meadow Road, turn left again on Marsh Street, and go to Main Street.

Rochambeau in 1781 to plan the last campaigns of the Revolution. The Isaac Stevens House (1788), while more modest, has an interesting collection of children's clothes and paraphernalia. Don't neglect to take note of the nineteenth-century elegance of the Capt. Hurbert House across the street from the Stevens House.

Now proceed to the intersection with Church Street and turn left. Go uphill. Cross the Silas Deane Highway. Go uphill again to Walcott Hill Road; turn left. At the crest of the hill cross Wells Road and go downhill to Prospect Street. Turn left at Prospect and then right into Millwoods Park. Here you may picnic but no longer swim. Alas, the town has changed to a Residents Only policy. In the picnic area on the other side of the pond there are some restrooms.

After visiting Millwoods Park, turn left onto Prospect Street, ride uphill to Ridge Road and turn right. The road crests at Wells Street. You will start downhill after crossing Rutledge. Turn right on Nott Street, where, after a brief uphill spurt, you get a nice downhill run. Cross the Silas Deane Highway again, go to Garden Street, the last street on your left before Hartford Avenue, and turn left. Cross Hartford Avenue and go in the entrance driveway to the Solomon Wells House (1774), which is now used only for local functions. The expanse of lawn down to the cove is a good picnic spot, however. When you're ready to leave, turn left on Hartford Avenue, which will lead you to Main Street and your car.

Pomfret

Number of miles: 15
Approximate pedalling time: 2 hours
Terrain: varied, some of it quite demanding
Surface: good
Things to see: Pomfret School, Annhurst College, Woodstock, Bowen Mansion, Roseland Park and Lake, Wappaquassett Pond, one-room schoolhouse

There are places in Pomfret and Woodstock where time seems to have passed very slowly. Come see. Start the ride at the Pomfret Post Office, which is located on Route 44 just east of the junctions of Routes 44 and 169. Return to the junction, then turn right onto 169 north, which is a real rollercoaster of a hill as you leave town. In 2 miles you'll pass through the campus of Annhurst College. Watch for a historical marker on the right between the college and the town of Woodstock. It designates the oldest one-room schoolhouse in America, which was built in 1748. It is located just off the road. At about the 3-mile mark, you will come to a stop sign, where Route 171 crosses 169. Turn left and continue on 169 to Woodstock. You will see a pink Victorian mansion on the left. This is the Bowen Mansion, which is open to the public and is well worth a visit.

Leaving Woodstock, take a right on Child's Hill Road at the end of the Green and ride downhill for a fast, magnificent 1½-mile run. At the bottom of the hill turn right onto Roseland Park Road at the stop sign. In a mile you'll enter the park on your left. Roseland Park was endowed by Henry Bowen of the pink mansion in Woodstock, and it has retained its fond turn-of-the-century ambiance. The park's golf

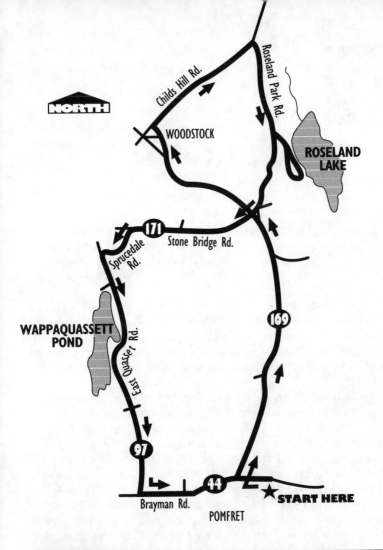

HOW to get there Pomfret is a few miles west of Putnam. From the south, take I–395 to Exit 93 (Killingly Center), then take Route 101 west to Route 169, and turn north to Pomfret.

From the west, take Route 86 to Exit 100, and take Route 44 east to Pomfret.

course, built in 1891, is said to be the oldest in the United States. Here you can picnic on the soft, sloping bank of the pond—a lovely, tranquil place. Head back to the road and turn left to resume your ride.

Turn right at Stone Bridge Road at the Common in South Woodstock. Cross Route 169. Now you face a real gear-shifter of a hill. Watch for Sprucedale Road on the left. Turn forty-five degrees onto Sprucedale, which soon forms a tee with East Quasset Road. Turn left on East Quasset and go up a steep hill, to the left, at the fork with West Quasset, past the cemetery to the top of the ridge. Wappaquassett Pond is on your right. Along this 2½-mile stretch there is one of the finest sights of this (or any other) ride: a winding country road, rolling meadows bounded by stone walls, cows, huge trees—all the ingredients of your favorite New England calendar! East Quasset Road comes to a tee at Brayman Road (Route 97); turn left. Here you have a mighty hill to master to regain Pomfret on the ridge. Cross Route 169 and return to the post office.

14

Storrs—
University of Connecticut

Number of miles:	12
Approximate pedalling time:	1½ hours
Terrain:	definitely hilly
Surface:	good
Things to see:	the University of Connecticut, an old stone mill, tumbling streams, and lovely countryside throughout

The University of Connecticut, unlike Yale, which is older but not necessarily wiser, has its campus out in the countryside where it has *room*. It's a beautiful campus, as is the area around it. As you drive along Route 195 on your way to the starting place at Dog Lane, look for the University Information Centers that are on 195 and stop for a campus map and places to see, such as the William Benton Art Museum.

The best place to start the ride is from Dog Lane, which is just past the main part of the campus, the first light after Mansfield Road and its stop sign. Coming from the direction of I–84, you'd turn left and park behind the Universal Store.

Mount up and turn left on Dog Lane. Go downhill about ¾ mile to the place where Dog Lane ends at a T intersection; turn right. In about ½ mile you'll come to a stop sign; continue straight ahead. You'll be on Hanks Hill Road, which has come in from the right at the stop sign. You were on Farrell Road (as you must know by now, in Connecticut roads change names or merge into others without warning!).

After another ½ mile you will come to the fork of Hanks Hill Road and Stone Hill Road. Bear right, staying on Hanks Hill. Just past the fork, at the mill pond, there is a sign that states, HERE ON HANKS

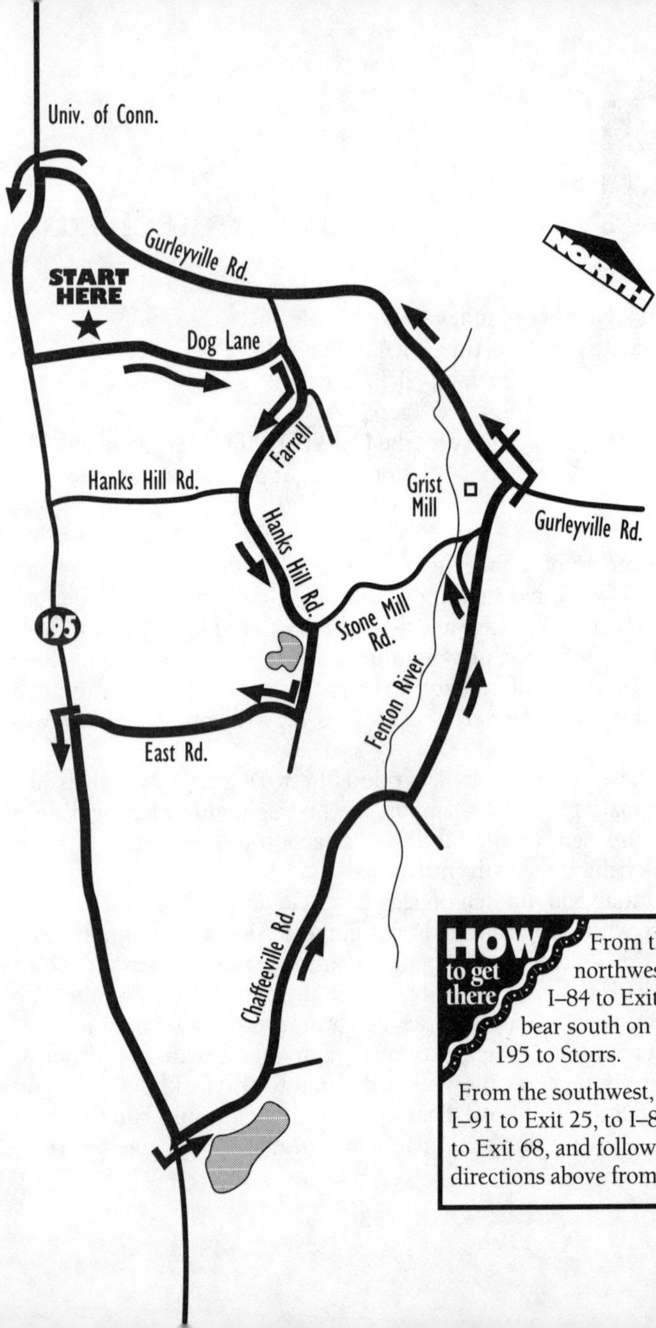

Univ. of Conn.

Gurleyville Rd.

START HERE

Dog Lane

Farrell

Hanks Hill Rd.

Hanks Hill Rd.

Grist Mill

Gurleyville Rd.

Stone Mill Rd.

Fenton River

195

East Rd.

Chaffeeville Rd.

NORTH

HOW to get there From the northwest, take I–84 to Exit 68; bear south on Route 195 to Storrs.

From the southwest, take I–91 to Exit 25, to I–84 east, to Exit 68, and follow the directions above from there.

HILL IN 1810 THE FIRST SILK MILL IN AMERICA WAS BUILT BY RODNEY HANKS. The mill itself is not here because it was removed lock, stone, and board by Henry Ford for his Dearborn Museum.

In another ½ mile, turn right. There's no road sign, but it is East Road. This is a very steep uphill, but there is a grand view at the crest where you can take a rest before turning left onto Route 195 and starting, shortly, a mile-long downhill run. As you tear along, look over to your left and you will see a stunning view of the hills. At the bottom of the hill you continue on the flat for another mile until you come to the intersection of Route 195 and Chaffeeville Road. Turn left onto Chaffeeville, which meanders for 3 miles through the countryside and then curves alongside a little river. Look for a sign, STONE MILL RD.—GRIST MILL, on the left side and a road going steeply down to the river (Stone Mill Road). Take it and you will come upon a serene scene: a narrow stretch of bottom land, a small cheerful river, and an old stone mill. This is the spot for a picnic!

The mill, built around 1830, is open on Sundays from noon to 4:00 P.M., mid-May to mid-October, and is the state's only remaining stone grist mill.

When you are ready, rejoin Chaffeeville Road and continue on to the next intersection where Chaffeeville, Gurleyville, and Codfish Falls roads meet. Turn left onto Gurleyville. After a short stretch the road starts steeply uphill but soon levels off and then snakes around an enormous meadow as it returns to Route 195 in the middle of the University of Connecticut campus. Here you can make a tour of the campus, or you can turn left onto 195 and ride about ½ mile back to your starting place.

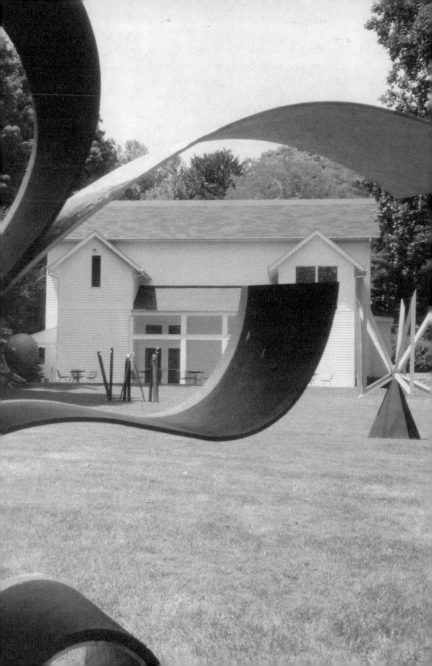

Ridgefield

Number of miles:	12
Approximate pedalling time:	2 hours
Terrain:	definitely hilly
Surface:	good
Things to see:	Ridgefield itself, Aldrich Museum of Contemporary Art, Lake Mamanasco

Ridgefield, like Litchfield and Farmington, is a small, beautifully preserved town full of revolutionary period history, and parts of it, except for the paved roads and automobiles, look much as they did in 1780.

Start your tour by beginning with the most modern piece of the town, the Aldrich Museum of Contemporary Art, which is on the right side of Main Street, just past the fountain and the point where Route 102 comes into Main. The museum shares the parking lot of the handsome church next door, and you can leave your car there. The contemporary sculpture is displayed in an outdoor garden. When you're ready to ride, turn right onto Main Street and proceed through the shopping area. If the traffic is heavy, use the broad sidewalk. Turn right at Prospect Street, at the third traffic light. When you come to East Ridge Road, turn right and go uphill. The road soon levels off, then goes downhill to a T intersection with Route 102. Turn right to return to Main Street. Turn left at Main, then right at the fountain where Route 35 joins Main Street. After you pass the Inn at Ridgefield, turn right onto Parley Lane, which angles off at forty-five degrees, then turn immediately right again onto High Ridge Road. Go to the junction of High Ridge and King Lane; continue on High Ridge by snaking left and immediately right. At Catoonah Street turn right and return to Main Street, where you should turn left.

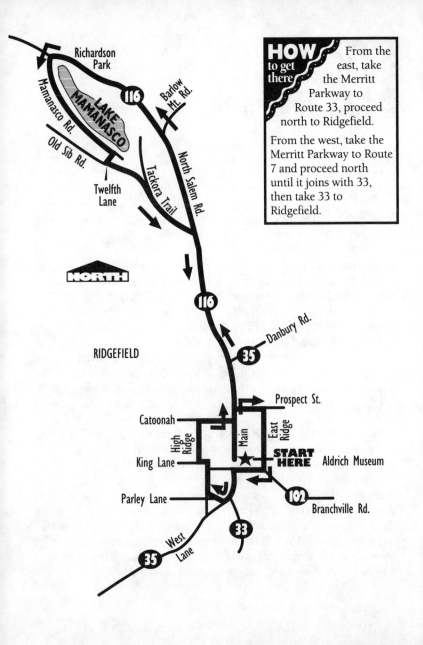

Richardson Park

LAKE MAMANASCO

Mamanasco Rd.

Old Sib Rd.

116

Barlow Mt. Rd.

Twelfth Lane

Tackora Trail

North Salem Rd.

NORTH

RIDGEFIELD

116

Danbury Rd.

35

Prospect St.

Catoonah

High Ridge

Main

East Ridge

King Lane

★ START HERE   Aldrich Museum

Parley Lane

102

Branchville Rd.

West Lane

33

35

HOW to get there

From the east, take the Merritt Parkway to Route 33, proceed north to Ridgefield.

From the west, take the Merritt Parkway to Route 7 and proceed north until it joins with 33, then take 33 to Ridgefield.

Just past the Elms Inn (which has been in continuous operation since 1799) is the site of the Battle of Ridgefield. In 1777, 600 militiamen under the command of Generals Wooster and Arnold attempted to cut off 1,800 British troops. Wooster was killed, and Arnold and his men finally withdrew as they were outflanked. There is a marker here inscribed: "On April 27, 1777, died 8 patriots who were laid in these grounds companioned by sixteen British soldiers, living their enemies, dying their guests."

The route for the next 4 miles to Lake Mamanasco is mostly downhill (but remember it will be uphill on the way back). When you come to a Y intersection, bear left on Route 116. Watch for the entrance to Richardson Park on the left. This wooded property is open to the public for hiking and picnicking. Turn left onto Mamanasco Road (across from the high school tennis courts). You are about 7 miles into the ride here. This route skirts the beautiful lake.

Turn right at Twelfth Lane at the end of the lake. You'll have to push up this one. At the top of the hill turn left on Old Sib Road, which soon joins Tackora Trail. Bear right on Route 116 at the junction and head back to town. Do stop at the Keeler Tavern (1733) at 133 Main Street. The tavern has been meticulously restored and is open on Wednesdays, weekends, and Monday holidays, from 1:00 to 4:00 P.M. It is truly a must see! Then on to your starting place at the Aldrich Museum.

Rowayton

Number of miles:	8½
Approximate pedalling time:	1 hour
Terrain:	one gradual hill and one very steep climb, otherwise flat
Surface:	fair
Things to see:	Tokeneke (Darien), Wilson Cove, the Sound, village of Rowayton, Three Mile River

Rowayton is one of the many picturesque small towns that wrap themselves around the fingers of land that make up most of Connecticut's long coastline and anchor or moor boats wherever there's enough water to float them.

We'll start in Darien from the parking lot of the Tokeneke School, which is just off Route 136 (Tokeneke Road). From the parking lot, turn left on Old Farm Road. The area of Tokeneke is dotted with huge houses and equally extravagant NO TRESPASSING signs, but the public roads provide a sufficient glimpse of manorial life. At the T intersection turn left onto Searles Road and right on Five Mile River Road, which reveals a view of the little village of Rowayton on the other side of the river (which is jammed with yachts). Five Mile River Road dead-ends at a turnaround bordered by a stone wall. Turn around and head back up the road. When the road forms a tee with Old Farm Road, turn right for a short distance to Tokeneke Road, where you turn right again and cross the bridge into Rowayton. Here the name of the road changes to Cudlipp. At the first light take a sharp left onto Rowayton Avenue. Go gradually uphill several blocks. Turn right on Devil's Garden Road, the fourth road after the railroad

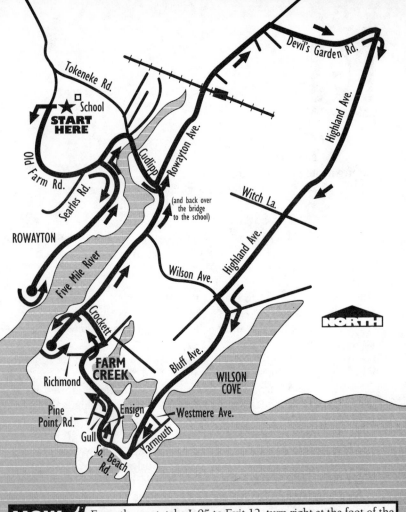

Tokeneke Rd.

School
★ START HERE

Old Farm Rd.

Searles Rd.

ROWAYTON

Five Mile River

Cudlipp

Rowayton Ave.

(and back over the bridge to the school)

Devil's Garden Rd.

Highland Ave.

Witch La.

Highland Ave.

Wilson Ave.

NORTH

Crockett

FARM CREEK

Richmond

Pine Point Rd.

Ensign

Westmere Ave.

Gull

Yarmouth

So. Beach Rd.

Bluff Ave.

WILSON COVE

HOW to get there From the west, take I–95 to Exit 12, turn right at the foot of the ramp, cross Locust Hill Road, and turn right in about ½ block into the parking lot of the Tokeneke School, where you may park.

From the east, take I–95 to Exit 11, turn right at the bottom of the ramp and go to Route 136 (before the railroad underpass), and turn right onto 136 (Tokeneke Road); continue on 136 until you come to Old Farm Road on the right; turn right, cross Locust Hill Road, and pull into the parking lot behind the school.

underpass. You'll go steeply uphill now until Devil's Garden forms a tee with Highland Avenue; turn right. At the second stop sign, turn left onto Wilson Avenue and go ½ block to Bluff Avenue.

Turn right on Bluff. You'll enjoy the downhill ride back to sea level, where there is a treat in store: you cross over a small bridge at Wilson Cove and from this vantage you can see Bell and Tavern islands and Wilson Point. Bluff changes its name to Westmere when it crosses the bridge; continue straight ahead. As you get close to the water you come to a stop sign where Yarmouth Road comes in at an angle from the left. Bear right and then right again onto South Beach Road, formerly Crescent Beach Road, from the shape of this fine little private beach. Continue on as the road goes right as Ensign Road, then turn left on Gull Street and right onto Pine Point Road and left at the T with Nearwater. In short order you'll bear right where Richmond comes in from the left, and then after a mercifully short distance you turn left onto Crockett Street, which will lead you to Rowayton Avenue, the village's main thoroughfare.

Turn left so you can explore the eastern end of Rowayton Avenue and the boat yards, then turn around and enjoy the flavor of the village as you pass its appealing yards, yacht brokerages, shops, and restaurants. Stay on Rowayton Avenue until you come to the light marking the intersection with Cudlipp Street; bear left, go over the bridge into Darien, and return to Old Farm Road and the Tokeneke School.

Shelton—Lake Zoar

Number of miles:	22
Approximate pedalling time:	3 hours
Terrain:	very demanding on the west side of the river, easy riding on the east side good on Routes 110 and 34, only fair on 111
Things to see:	the Housatonic River Valley, Derby and Shelton, Lake Zoar, Stevenson Dam, Monroe, Indian Well State Park

This 22-mile ride will take you from the Indian Well State Park, which borders the Housatonic River in Shelton, west to the little town of Monroe and then north to Lake Zoar, down along its southern shore and across Stevenson Dam, which created the lake, to the east bank of the river. Perhaps the land alongside a river is called a bank rather than a shore because it usually slopes upward or "banks" away from the river. Whatever the reason, you should be in good condition before you take this ride, because you will have several long uphill climbs before you get to the downhill runs.

Start from Indian Well State Park, which is about 2 miles up Route 110 from Shelton. At the sign INDIAN WELL STATE PARK, turn right and park in the first parking lot. Don't go down to the lower, beach area of the road; it dead-ends there, and you'd have a long uphill climb back up to the entrance of the park. Figure on a refreshing swim down there in the placid Housatonic River when you finish the ride. (Did you know that *Housatonic* means "place beyond the mountains" in Algonquin?)

At the entrance to the park turn right onto Route 110 and start

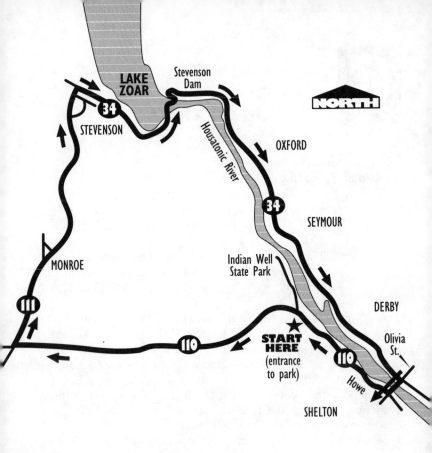

LAKE ZOAR

Stevenson Dam

NORTH

34

STEVENSON

Housatonic River

OXFORD

34

SEYMOUR

Indian Well State Park

DERBY

MONROE

111

Olivia St.

★ START HERE
(entrance to park)

110

110

Howe

SHELTON

HOW to get there   From the west, take the Merritt Parkway to Exit 52 (Route 8), turn north on Route 8, get off at Exit 14, follow signs to Shelton on Route 110 to Indian Well State Park, 2 miles north of Shelton.

From the east, take Route 34 to Shelton, turn right after crossing the bridge (Route 110) and proceed north to the park.

climbing. Here is where a modified mountain bike with twenty-one gear combinations would prove its worth! There are several long inclines, including a 1½-mile grind at the start. Stay on Route 110 as it turns west, away from the river, through sparsely settled country to Route 111, about 5 miles from the start of your ride.

Turn right onto Route 111. This is a secondary road; the surface is irregular, and the shoulders aren't clearly marked. In about ½ mile you'll come to the town of Monroe with its tiny green and massive trees, flanked by handsome old houses and churches. It was in this vicinity that the Comte de Rochambeau's French army of four divisions encamped on their march from Newport, Rhode Island, to Yorktown for the last and decisive battle of the Revolutionary War.

Continue on Route 111 out of Monroe, a nice run, mostly downhill, to the junction with Route 34; turn right for a brief ride along Lake Zoar to the Stevenson Dam. There's a drive-in restaurant on the right just after you turn onto Route 34, and just before you cross over the dam, you'll see Zoar Beach, which is open to the public. The road over the dam is quite narrow, so stick close to the right. On the other side of the dam there's a large restaurant on your left overlooking the lake.

Turn right here and ride down Route 34 along the border of the lake—at times close to its "bank." As you approach Derby, you might see the long, thin racing shells of Yale University practicing or racing up and down the river. One recent spring day I saw nine of them followed by their chase boats. They were evidently holding a regatta. This section of Route 34 is called Roosevelt Drive, and you pass through parts of Oxford, Seymour, and finally Derby, where you turn right at Olivia Street and go over the bridge into Shelton, taking a right onto Route 110 (Howe Avenue) for the 2-mile ride back to Indian Well State Park and a well-deserved picnic or swim.

Stratford—Lordship

Number of miles:	12½
Approximate pedalling time:	1½ hours
Terrain:	flat
Surface:	mostly good, some poor paving
Things to see:	Judson House Museum, American Shakespeare Festival Theater, Bridgeport Airport, Long Island Sound at Lordship

There is much to see and do on this ride along the mouth of the Housatonic and the shores of Long Island Sound, so begin on West Broad Street if you are here on a weekend or from Academy Hill Road if you should come on a weekday.

Ride the short distance to the T intersection with Main Street; turn right and then left onto Academy Hill Road. On your right halfway up the brief hill stands the Judson House Museum (1723), which is open on Wednesdays, Saturdays, and Sundays from 11:00 A.M. to 5:00 P.M. There is a small fee.

At the top of Academy Hill turn right onto Elm Street. When you come to the entrance of the American Festival Theater, turn into the grounds. In England this ride might be called Stratford on Housatonic—Lordship on the Sound. In any case, twenty some years ago, because our Stratford was also on a river and in Connecticut where many theater people reside and so forth, an enlarged version of Shakespeare's Globe Theater was built on the shores of Stratford on Housatonic and called the Stratford Shakespeare Theater. It was a marvelous spot for a picnic before the performance, on the lawn, under a tall shady tree overlooking the river, and it still is today but

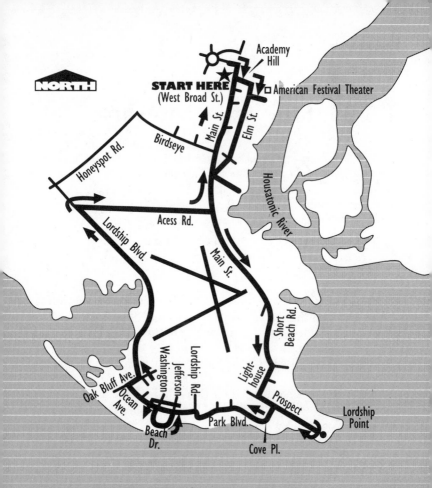

NORTH

Academy Hill

START HERE
(West Broad St.)

□ American Festival Theater

Birdseye

Main St.

Elm St.

Honeyspot Rd.

Housatonic River

Acess Rd.

Lordship Blvd.

Main St.

Short Beach Rd.

Oak Bluff Ave.

Ocean Ave.

Jefferson

Washington

Lordship Rd.

Lighthouse

Prospect

Lordship Point

Beach Dr.

Park Blvd.

Cove Pl.

HOW to get there
From the east and west, take I–95 to Exit 32 at Stratford and go to West Broad Street.

From the north, take Route 8 to Route 108, go south on 108 to Route 1, cross 1, and bear right on North Parade Street; turn right on Main Street, go under the turnpike, and go to West Broad Street.

the theater is now called the American Festival Theater and is closed for renovations.

On leaving the theater, turn left on Elm Street. In a few blocks, after you pass Tide Harbor condominiums, there is a stop sign; turn left again and ride down to the launching area to watch the boats. Return to Elm Street and turn left. Elm forms a tee with Main; turn left. You are now on Stratford Point. After passing the airport you'll come to a Y; take the left fork, which is Short Beach Road. A short distance down this road is a new state park on the left, the Short Beach Road State Park. Turn in and take a look around. There's a beach for swimming and picnic benches under the trees and a snack bar.

When you come back to the entrance, turn left and ride to Lighthouse Avenue, the last road on the right before the dead end (it may not be marked); turn right. Lighthouse comes to a tee at Prospect Drive. Turn left here and proceed to the lighthouse, then turn around and ride back down Prospect to Cove Place on your left. Turn left onto Cove and ride a short stretch to the Sound, where you turn right onto Park Boulevard.

Park Boulevard ends when it forms a tee with Lordship Road. Turn right and immediately left on Ocean Avenue. Then turn left again on Washington Parkway. Washington Parkway makes a T with Beach Drive; go left. There is a sea wall here bounded by giant rocks to climb over, fish from, and sit on; and there are a couple of restaurants facing the water. After your R and R at the water's edge, continue on Beach Drive heading east. Turn left on Ocean Avenue and proceed until it forms a tee at Oak Bluff Avenue. Turn right. When Oak Bluff intersects with Lordship, turn left. You will now cross a great salt marsh. Ride past the airport with the World War II Navy gull wing fighter plane standing guard. If you're ready for a rest stop, there are restrooms in the terminal.

Continue until you come to the traffic light where Acess Road intersects. Turn right, ride to the T with Main Street, and turn left onto Main and ride back to your starting place on either Academy Hill Road or West Broad Street.

Branford

Number of miles:	14
Approximate pedalling time:	2 hours
Terrain:	flat to moderately hilly
Surface:	good
Things to see:	The Blackstone Memorial Library, Branford Green, Bruce and Johnson Marina, Stony Creek, Thimble Islands, Puppet House Theater

Branford is one of the eleven shoreline towns that hug the coast from New Haven to the Rhode Island border, and a lovely old town it is, well worth exploring.

Park near the town hall on the Green and ride west on Main Street the short distance to the Blackstone Library on your right. Be sure to go into the auditorium at the rear of the first floor and see this Victorian gem. When you leave the library, turn left toward the green and angle off almost immediately forty-five degrees to the right at the fork onto South Main Street; ride down past the sign SCENIC DRIVE to the T intersection with Montowese Street, and turn right onto what is also Route 146. Follow 146 as it goes under the Amtrak overpass, over the upper end of the Branford River to a big stop sign where Indian Neck Avenue comes in from the right and joins forces with Montowese. Continue around a slight bend to the left about ½ mile till you come to Block Island Road on the right. Turn right *only* if you like to look at boats. Once back to Indian Neck–Montowese Road continue down to a Y where you bear left and then ninety degrees left at the water for a short ride along the shore. As the road starts to turn inland be alert for the Connecticut sport, "fool the tourist by chang-

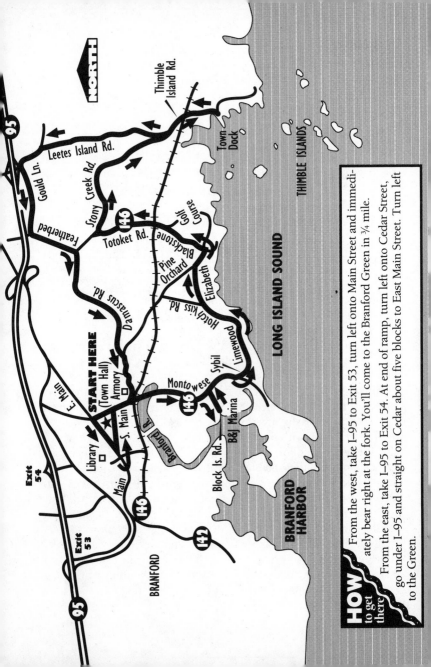

NORTH

I-95

Exit 54

Exit 53

BRANFORD

142

146

Main

E. Main

Library

S. Main

START HERE
(Town Hall)

Armory

146

Montowese

Block Is. Rd.

B&J Marina

Sybil

Branford

Damascus Rd.

Featherbed

Gould Ln.

Leetes Island Rd.

Stony Creek Rd.

146

Totoket Rd.

Pine Orchard

Blackstone

Golf Course

Elizabeth

Hotchkiss Rd.

Limewood

Thimble Island Rd.

Town Dock

THIMBLE ISLANDS

LONG ISLAND SOUND

BRANFORD HARBOR

HOW to get there   From the west, take I-95 to Exit 53, turn left onto Main Street and immediately bear right at the fork. You'll come to the Branford Green in ¾ mile.

From the east, take I-95 to Exit 54. At end of ramp, turn left onto Cedar Street, go under I-95 and straight on Cedar about five blocks to East Main Street. Turn left to the Green.

ing street names." You've been on Limewood Avenue, which becomes Hotchkiss Grove Road, which you leave as it goes left and inland at a Y where Second Avenue is on your right. Bear right on what is now Elizabeth Street (which may not be marked!) and ride past six side streets to where Pine Orchard Road takes over, coming down from your left. Turn right and go the short distance to where you turn left onto Blackstone Avenue, which is also Route 146. Ride up Blackstone, with the Pine Orchard Golf Club on your right and Young's Pond on the left, to the Y intersection with Totoket Road; bear left. Ride under the railroad tracks and up Totoket (Route 146) about 3/4 mile to the Y intersection with what is called Damascus Road on the left and Stony Creek Road on the right. You are going to Stony Creek, so turn right. Stay on Stony Creek Road as it meanders for about 2 miles past the Wightwood School and the Trap Rock single-track railroad to the four-way intersection with Leetes Island and Thimble Island roads. Turn right and ride down Thimble Island Road into Stony Creek, a quirky waterfront village whose inhabitants call themselves "Creekers." Ride down to the town dock and prepare yourself for a truly unique treat, a forty-five-minute cruise through the Thimble Islands. From June 1 through September 8 there are daily cruises departing at quarter past the hour from 10:15 A.M. to 5:15 P.M. From May 4 through May 31 and September 9 to October 12, the cruises are on Friday, Saturday, and Sunday only. There are thirty-two tiny islands, all of which have fascinating histories.

As you ride back the way you came, stop and take a look inside the Stony Creek Puppet House Theater to see how the theater got its name. Several years ago one of your authors appeared on stage here with his son in Shaw's *Arms and the Man*. At the four-way intersection, ride straight ahead on Leetes Island Road to Gould Lane just before I–95. Turn left to the T with Featherbed Lane and left to a T with Damascus Road. Turn right following Damascus, bearing left at the intersection with Victoria down to the Y where you join Pine Orchard Road, bearing right to Montowese, where you turn right for the ride back to the green.

Chester—East Haddam

Number of miles:	14
Approximate pedalling time:	2 hours
Terrain:	fairly flat on the west side of the river, definitely hilly on the east side
Surface:	good
Things to see:	the Connecticut River, Gillette Castle, Goodspeed Opera House, Gelston House Restaurant, towns of Chester and East Haddam

There are many plusses on this ride: the five-minute ferry trip on the Chester–Hadlyme ferry, the Rhine River-like view from the terrace at Gillette Castle, the Victorian mood of the Goodspeed Opera House, the varied terrain, and, above all, the lively Connecticut River.

Park your car in Chester Center near the handsome stone building that stands at the principal intersection. (The building, incidentally, is *not* a courthouse; it is a package store!) Start by heading east on Route 148, crossing Route 154, to the Hadlyme Ferry. The ferry operates from April 1 to November 30 from 7:00 A.M. to 8:45 P.M. Bikes only cost 50 cents and don't have to wait in line. After crossing the river, proceed up the steep hill to the left for about a mile to Gillette Castle State Park. Be careful on this heavily travelled, narrow road. The castle, home of a wealthy actor from a bygone era, is ½ mile from the park's entrance.

Upon leaving the park, turn left. You will now have a very hilly ride to the intersection with Route 82 (Brush Hill Road), where you turn left. Continue bearing left on Route 82. In a little over a mile there will be a stop sign; turn sharply left (still on 82) and you will be

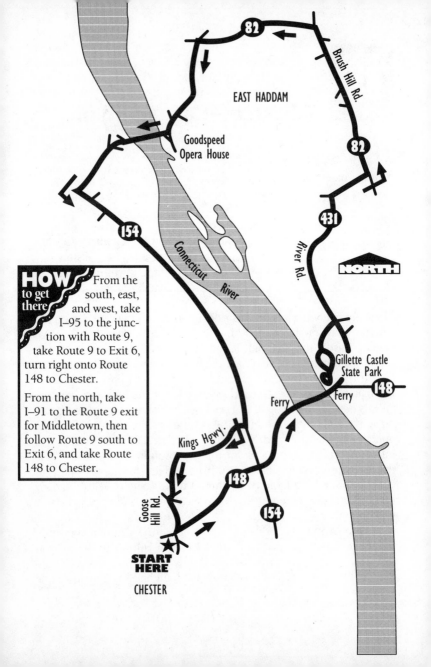

82

EAST HADDAM

Brush Hill Rd.

Goodspeed
Opera House

82

154

431

River Rd.

Connecticut River

NORTH

HOW to get there
From the south, east, and west, take I–95 to the junction with Route 9, take Route 9 to Exit 6, turn right onto Route 148 to Chester.

From the north, take I–91 to the Route 9 exit for Middletown, then follow Route 9 south to Exit 6, and take Route 148 to Chester.

Gillette Castle
State Park

148

Ferry

Ferry

Kings Hwy.

148

154

Goose Hill Rd.

START HERE

CHESTER

exhilarated by the 1-mile downhill into the town of East Haddam. While here be sure to visit the Goodspeed Opera House, lovingly and authentically restored in the 1960s; and take time to browse the attractive shops that line the streets. Be sure to pull off the road and watch the small airplanes landing on the strip nearby, or passengers boarding cruise ships for outings on the river and to Long Island. (In the last half of the 1800s steamboat traffic from New York to Hartford brought many fashionable people to the town.)

Upon leaving East Haddam, take the bridge over the river, riding on the solid area close to the railing. Turn left at the T intersection, complete with traffic light, of Routes 82 and 154 south. In about 3 miles, after passing Goose Hill Road on the right and the Susan Bates knitting needle factory on the left, you'll come to Kings Highway; turn right and go uphill to the T intersection with Goose Hill Road. Turn left. In about ½ mile bear left again, continuing on Goose Hill Road, which will take you downhill into Chester at the intersection where you left your car.

Essex

Number of miles:	13½
Approximate pedalling time:	2 hours
Terrain:	gentle to downright hilly
Surface:	good
Things to see:	Griswold Inn, the Connecticut River, several marinas, the Copper Beech Inn, Ivoryton Playhouse, and the Valley Railroad

Essex is one of the jewels in Connecticut's crown. It's a river town and mighty expensive to live in but a joy to visit. It's home to many authors, such as the novelist Brian Burland, and if you like sailboats or large power yachts—feast your eyes!

Begin by parking your car behind the Town Hall, just past the Route 9 overpass on Route 153 (West Avenue). Mount up and proceed downhill into Essex proper, passing the Pratt House and Smithy; bear around to the left, following the sign into Old Essex. Turn right at Main Street, and follow it, past the Griswold Inn, down to the river's edge. Here you will find a river full of large sailing yachts (boats this big are yachts!) and the River Museum at Steamboat Dock, an 1878 steamboat warehouse open Tuesday through Sunday 10:00 A.M. to 5:00 P.M.

Turn around and come up Main to Ferry Street; turn right. Ferry Street ends at the ferry slip (for a tiny ferry with fringe on top, which goes to the Essex Island Marina). After a look at all the dream boats, turn left on Pratt Street, head uphill to North Main Street, turn right, and within ½ mile you'll find a cemetery on your right. Go into the cemetery, down to the water's edge. This is a beautiful spot to rest.

HOW to get there

From the north, take Route 9 south to Exit 3, follow the signs on Route 153 into Essex.

From the east, take I–95 west to Exit 69 to Route 9 to Exit 3 and on into Essex.

From the west, take I–95 to Exit 65. Turn left onto Route 153 and follow it to Essex.

Return to North Main Street and turn right. In about 1 mile North Main becomes River Road. After another 2 miles you'll come to a stop sign at the juncture of River Road and Book Hill Road. Make the 160-degree turn left onto Book Hill Road. It's a steep hill, but after a mile the road goes as steeply downhill for a fine, free ride for ½ mile, until the T intersection of Book Hill and River roads. Turn right onto River Road and ride ¼ mile to the intersection of Dennison Road. Turn 45 degrees right onto Dennison, and you are on the road to Ivoryton, about 3 miles from this point.

Dennison takes you over Route 9 and then to the little town of Centerbrook. At the intersection of Dennison and Middlesex Turnpike, turn right and follow the signs to Ivoryton. Middlesex Turnpike will soon bear almost 90 degrees right. Continue straight on what is now Main Street, past the renowned Copper Beech Inn, into Ivoryton.

Check out the Ivoryton Playhouse and the tiny square, then double back on Main Street, passing Dennison Road, bearing right on Middlesex Turnpike, to the Valley Railroad, which is well worth a stop! Better yet, give it a couple of hours and ride the antique steam train to Deep River to board an authentic riverboat for an hour's cruise on one of America's most beautiful rivers, the Connecticut.

Continue on Middlesex Turnpike, downhill, under Route 9, and immediately left at the traffic light onto West Avenue. You are back in Essex, ⅓ mile from the Town Hall and your starting place.

Guilford

Number of miles:	20½
Approximate pedalling time:	2½ hours
Terrain:	mostly gentle, a couple of tough hills
Surface:	good
Things to see:	Guilford Green and harbor, Henry Whitfield House, Hyland House, Griswold House, Monastery of Our Lady of Grace

Guilford, one of Connecticut's shoreline towns, has over one hundred houses built in the eighteenth century and the oldest stone house in the United States, plus one of the prettiest Greens—as you will soon see. Begin in Guilford at the junction of I–95 and Route 77, where you can park in either of the two commuter parking lots on the north side of I–95. Ride south on Route 77. You are heading toward the Guilford Green and the sea. After about 1 mile, you'll come to the Green. This is one of the loveliest commons in New England. It is flanked by a spired white Congregational church, stately houses, and quaint shops. At the Green turn right onto Broad Street and then left on Whitfield Street, which will take you down to the Sound. In a mile you will see the striking Henry Whitfield House on the left. Built in 1639 with dense stone walls, a sixty-degree, sloping tiled roof, leaded windows, and twin chimneys, it is reputedly the oldest stone house in America. It is furnished with period pieces and is open to the public. It's a short ride to the house—for a long journey back in time, to the early Colonial days. Back in the present, ride over the railroad tracks for a sweeping view of the Sound and the reed-rich marshes, characteristic of the Connecticut shoreline. Proceed to the harbor past the

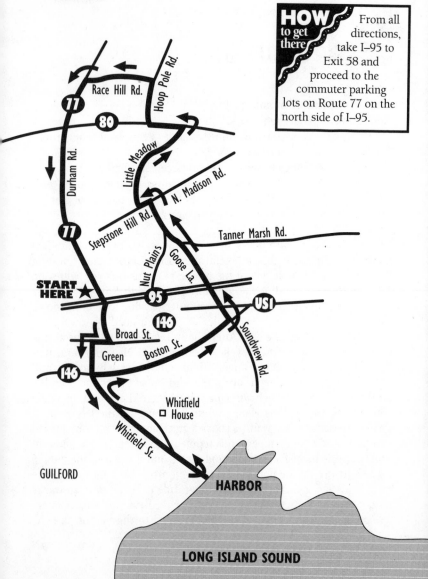

HOW to get there

From all directions, take I–95 to Exit 58 and proceed to the commuter parking lots on Route 77 on the north side of I–95.

NORTH

Race Hill Rd.

Hoop Pole Rd.

77

80

Durham Rd.

Little Meadow

N. Madison Rd.

Stepstone Hill Rd.

Tanner Marsh Rd.

77

Nut Plains

Goose La.

START HERE ★

95

US1

146

Broad St.

Green

Boston St.

Soundview Rd.

146

Whitfield □ House

Whitfield St.

GUILFORD

HARBOR

LONG ISLAND SOUND

Beecher House (1740). At the harbor there are three good restaurants to tempt you, or you can have a picnic sitting on the rocks at harborside.

On the return, ride up Whitfield, taking Old Whitfield for a short distance to bring you to the Henry Whitfield House (if you waited until now to see it). Old Whitfield brings you back to Whitfield Street. Proceed back to the Green. Turn right at the foot of the Green onto Boston Street (it may not be marked). Notice the Hyland House (1660) and the Griswold House (1735), both open to the public. Ride to Soundview Road. You are now approximately 9 miles from your starting point. Turn left, going under the turnpike.

Soundview becomes Goose Lane. In about a mile, Goose Lane turns left where Tanner Marsh Road comes in from the right. Continue on Goose Lane for about ½ mile to where Nut Plains Road comes in from the left. There is an old, small cemetery on the right; keep to the right. Goose Lane is now Nut Plains Road, which soon forms a tee with Stepstone Hill Road (to the right this road is called North Madison Road).

Go left up very steep Stepstone Hill Road and turn right near the top of the hill onto Little Meadow Road. Now you'll have a downhill swing on Little Meadow Road all the way to Route 80. (Bear right at the fork formed by Little Meadow and Hoop Pole roads.) When you reach Route 80, turn left and go uphill about ⁷⁄₁₀ mile to Hoop Pole Road. Turn right. After going uphill past ponds and woods, you'll come to Our Lady of Grace Monastery (Dominican nuns). Turn left here onto Race Hill Road. Turn left at the bottom of the hill onto Route 77 (Durham Road). When you come to the junction with Route 80, continue on Route 77, for about 4 miles, mostly downhill, to your starting place at Route 77 and I–95.

Killingworth

Number of miles:	13½
Approximate pedalling time:	2 hours
Terrain:	demanding
Surface:	good
Things to see:	Country Squire Inn and Antique Shop, several fine churches and houses, Chatfield Hollow State Park

This ride is out in the country, and it takes you through no towns, no villages, just beautiful countryside.

We didn't call this ride "Killingworth" because it will give you a good workout; there really is a township by that name. Seriously, if you are in good physical condition and ride a ten-, twelve-, or twenty-one-speed bicycle, you will enjoy yourself—especially the swim in Chatfield Hollow State Park at the end.

Begin by parking your car in the Park and Ride lot on the northwest corner of the junction of Routes 80 and 81. Head east on Route 80 toward Winthrop and Deep River. In about 2½ miles after an uphill and a downhill, you'll enter the township of Deep River, passing a lake and Route 145 south on your right. A little further up the road, about 4 miles into the ride, turn left on Route 145 north, which is little more than a country lane. (The sign to 145 north is practically hidden, but a country church on your left as you reach the crest of the hill marks the spot.)

Moderate up and downhill swings characterize the first part of this stretch on Route 145 north. You will ride through a Hobbit-like glen, where the tree-shaded road snakes right and left; no doubt Orcs dwell in this part of the forest. After about 2½ miles there is a sign to

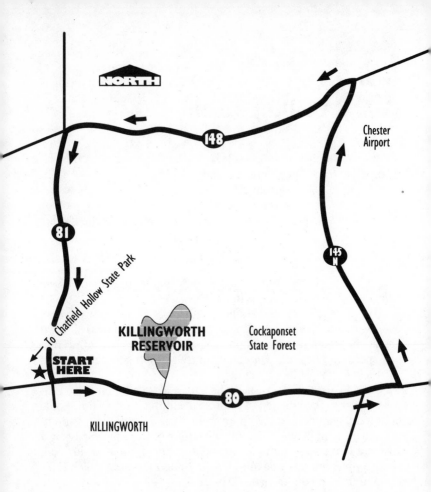

NORTH

148

Chester
Airport

81

To Chatfield Hollow State Park

**KILLINGWORTH
RESERVOIR**

Cockaponset
State Forest

145
N

★ **START
HERE**

80

KILLINGWORTH

HOW
*to get
there*   From the south, take I–95 to Exit 63;
head north on Route 81 to Route 80.

From the north, take Route 9 out of
Middletown to Exit 9; then head south on
Route 81 to Route 80.

Chester Airport. If you enjoy watching small planes take off and land, turn right up the brief hill to the field. There are restrooms also!

The difficult part of the ride comes when you turn left at the intersection of Routes 145 and 148. This leg of the ride is a grueling 3½ miles of uphill riding, all the way to Route 81. When you reach Route 81, turn left and head back to your starting point. Just before you get to the intersection of Routes 80 and 81, where you parked your car, take a look at Killingworth's perfect Congregational church on the left.

Before you head home, wrap up the day with a visit to Chatfield Hollow State Park, which is only a mile to the west on Route 80 from where your car is parked. Bike or drive down the rollercoaster hill to the park, where you can swim and picnic and enjoy the coolness of the hollow after your workout.

Madison–Hammonasset

Number of miles: 17
Approximate pedalling time: 2½ hours
Terrain: flat to slightly hilly
Surface: good
Things to see: the shoreline town of Madison with its exceptional Congregational church, Hammonasset State Park

Madison is often called a bedroom town for New Haven, but only by those who don't live there. It not only is a beautiful New England small town but also has within its borders Hammonasset State Park, the largest beach in Connecticut—and a favorite place for walks along the beach in the spring, fall, and winter.

The best place to start from is the commuter Park and Ride lot on Goose Lane (exit 59 off I–95) in Guilford. When you're ready to ride, turn right from the parking lot, go under I–95 to the intersection with Route 1, and turn left. One mile into the ride brings you to the East River. Here there are marshes on both sides of the road, and you'll enjoy a lovely view of the Sound. About ½ mile from the East River, turn left onto Wildwood Avenue, which takes you through the country part of Madison, fine in the summer and even better in the fall. The road snakes around to the right and forks; take the right fork. Your road becomes Green Hill. Soon you pass Nortontown Road. The Munger Lumber Company suddenly appears, and then another fork; bear right. The road starts uphill at this point, levels off as you pass Copse Road, and then goes briefly uphill again.

At the 4-mile point Green Hill crosses Route 79. Continue on Green Hill, which curves around and down to the intersection with

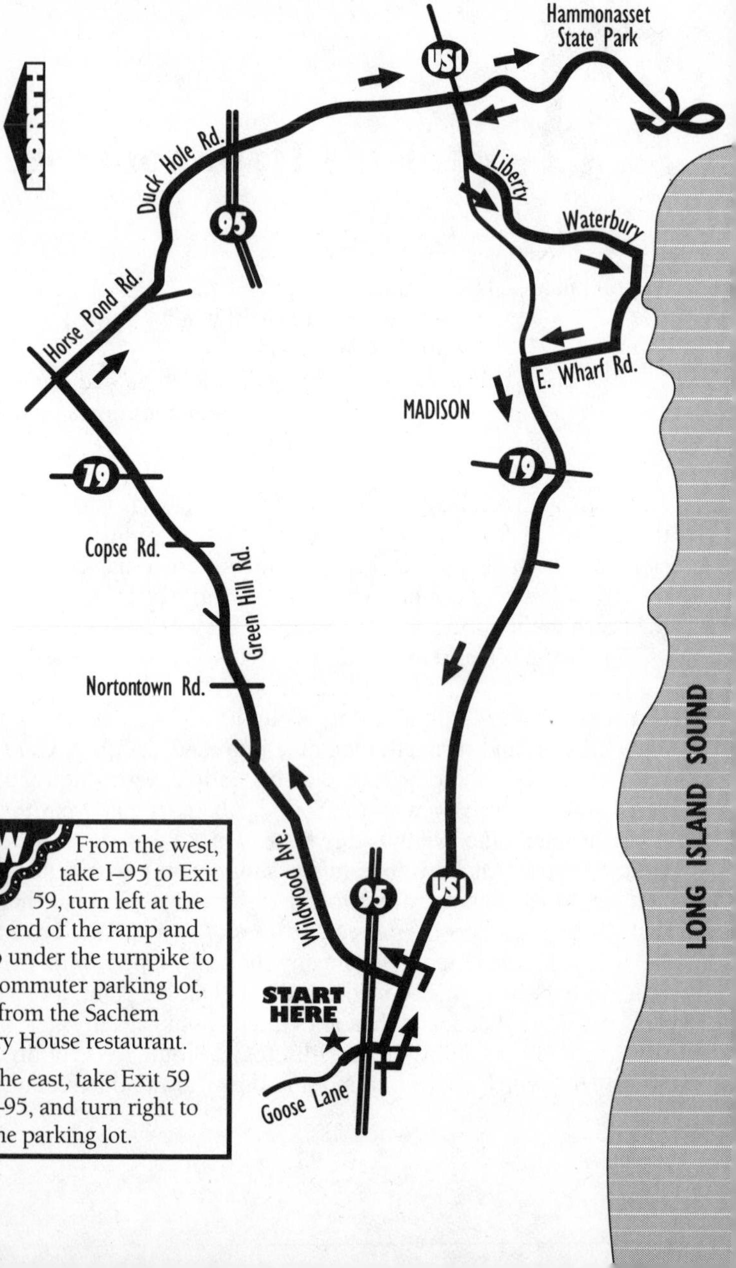

NORTH

Hammonasset State Park

US1

Duck Hole Rd.

95

Liberty

Waterbury

Horse Pond Rd.

E. Wharf Rd.

MADISON

79

79

Copse Rd.

Green Hill Rd.

Nortontown Rd.

Wildwood Ave.

95

US1

HOW to get there   From the west, take I–95 to Exit 59, turn left at the end of the ramp and go under the turnpike to the commuter parking lot, across from the Sachem Country House restaurant.

From the east, take Exit 59 from I–95, and turn right to go to the parking lot.

START HERE

Goose Lane

LONG ISLAND SOUND

Horse Pond Road. Turn right onto Horse Pond, which has a wide shoulder. Within 1½ miles Horse Pond goes off to the right; continue straight on your present road, which becomes Duck Hole Road. At the intersection of Duck Hole with Route 1, there is a traffic light at the bottom of a hill. Cross over and enter Hammonasset State Park. You will find 2 miles of sandy beach, complete with dressing and restrooms, and snack bars (open only in the summer), as well as a boardwalk—all part of a 919-acre state park. Lock your bikes and have a swim and/or a picnic or just a leisurely stroll along the beautiful, white sand beach.

Come back out to Route 1 and turn left. The road goes gently up and down, and at the bottom of the third hill there is a caution light. Turn left onto Liberty Street. At Waterbury Avenue turn left and ride down to the shore for an uncluttered view of the Sound. Turn right at the stop sign at East Wharf Road. Soon East Wharf forms a tee with Route 1. Turn left and go through the brief but well-manicured shopping section.

After passing the intersection of Routes 79 and 1 (Main Street), you will come upon the Green. Bear right and loop around the Green, passing in front of the magnificent First Congregational Church, built in 1707. Return to Route 1 and continue on it past West Wharf Road and the cemetery. Return to Goose Lane in Guilford and your starting place.

New Haven—East Rock

Number of miles:	9
Approximate pedalling time:	1¼ hours
Terrain:	flat in the city, then up and down fabulous East Rock
Surface:	good
Things to see:	New Haven Green, New Haven Colony Historical Society, Peabody Museum, East Rock Park and THE VIEW, Lake Whitney, Edgerton Park

This is a spectacular 9-mile circuit from the New Haven Green to the summit of East Rock and back. You won't believe you did it until you reach the top of East Rock, 365 feet above the plain, and suddenly see all of the city and surrounding countryside, the harbor, and Long Island Sound below you! Note that the summit is closed from November 1 till April 1, *except* from 8:00 A.M.–4:00 P.M. on Saturdays, Sundays, and holidays.

The ride begins at the corner of Elm and Church streets at the Green. Head north on Church Street. In 2 blocks you will notice that Church changes its name to Whitney Avenue—it's a fine old New England custom.

At the corner of Sachem and Whitney, you'll pass the Peabody Museum of Natural History, which is well worth a long visit, and other buildings of Yale University. Proceed to Edwards Street. Take a right on Edwards and a left onto Livingston. At the corner of Cold Spring Street and Livingston, you will find yourself at College Woods, a part of East Rock Park. Proceed straight to East Rock Road. Turn right and cross the Mill River. Dead ahead you'll confront 365 feet of

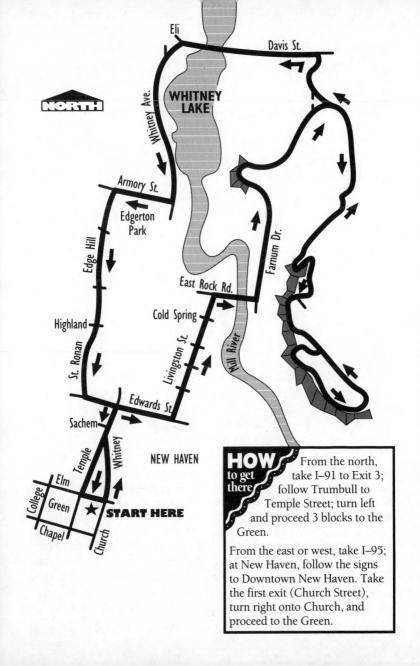

NORTH

Eli

Davis St.

WHITNEY LAKE

Whitney Ave.

Armory St.

Edgerton Park

Edge Hill

East Rock Rd.

Cold Spring

Highland

Livingston St.

Farnum Dr.

Mill River

St. Ronan

Edwards St.

Sachem

Temple

Whitney

NEW HAVEN

Elm

College

Green

★ START HERE

Chapel

Church

HOW to get there From the north, take I–91 to Exit 3; follow Trumbull to Temple Street; turn left and proceed 3 blocks to the Green.

From the east or west, take I–95; at New Haven, follow the signs to Downtown New Haven. Take the first exit (Church Street), turn right onto Church, and proceed to the Green.

stone: the near-vertical face of East Rock. Turn left onto Farnum Drive to begin your gradual climb. Farnum Drive makes a long loop to the meadow on the north and then snakes its way to the summit, which has several great spots for picnicking.

The ride down is heavenly! Take the same route, bearing right after passing through the gate, then turning left when Farnum comes to a T at Davis Street. Cross the bridge over Lake Whitney, and bear left at the intersection formed by Eli and Davis streets. Ride a few yards up the hill to the traffic light on Whitney Avenue; turn left.

At the next traffic light turn right onto Armory Street. The property on the left, which resembles a fortification from Quebec, is, in fact, a storage facility of the New Haven Water Company. The little house on the corner (1799) was a boarding house for Eli Whitney's gun factory. Go 1 block to Edgehill Road and turn left. At number 145 Edgehill, on the left, there is a secret garden, Edgerton Park—a walled park of several rolling acres, which is open to all. There is also a mystery: Where is the mansion of the estate? Alas, it was destroyed at the stipulation of the donors in their will.

Edgehill becomes St. Ronan when you cross Highland. When St. Ronan forms a tee with Edwards Street, turn left and go downhill to Whitney, where you turn right. Best to take the sidewalk here. Whitney forks at the mini-park at Trumbull Street; bear right. Cross Elm and take a short tour of New Haven's picturesque Green before returning to your car.

New Haven—Sleeping Giant

Number of miles:	25
Approximate pedalling time:	3½ hours
Terrain:	hilly
Surface:	mostly good, some rough spots
Things to see:	New Haven Green, Yale University, Sleeping Giant State Park, John Dickerman House, Quinnipiac College, Hamden

New Haven needs no introduction, but you may not be familiar with the Sleeping Giant. The best vantage point to see him from is on I–91 heading north out of New Haven. As you approach Exit 8, look ahead and to the left and there he is, sleeping on his back, about 2 miles long from his head to his feet!

Start your ride from College Street at the Green. Go to the archway called Phelps Gate in the center of the block-long Yale University building, which flanks College Street. Ride through the arch and across the Old Campus to High Street. Turn right and go to Grove. (If the gate to Old Campus is closed, go left on College to Chapel, then right 1 block to High and right to Grove.) This is the heart of the university. Turn left on Grove and curve past the gymnasium (largest in the world, per Mr. Guinness) to the traffic light. Be careful here. Bear right past Dixwell and Goffe, and turn right on Whalley Avenue.

Proceed out Whalley, which bears to the right 2⅖ miles from the start at the junction of Routes 243 and 63 (Whalley is 63). In another mile you will come to the **Y** intersection of 63 and 69; bear right onto 69. Within ½ mile you'll find yourself on a two-lane country road, which takes you uphill past farms and a lovely lake. A mile past the

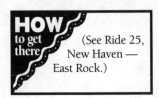

HOW to get there (See Ride 25, New Haven — East Rock.)

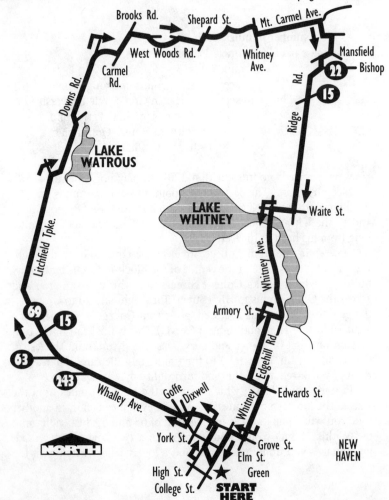

Sleeping Giant State Park

Brooks Rd.

Shepard St.

Mt. Carmel Ave.

West Woods Rd.

Whitney Ave.

Mansfield

Carmel Rd.

Bishop

22

15

Downs Rd.

Ridge Rd.

LAKE WATROUS

LAKE WHITNEY

Waite St.

Litchfield Tpke.

Whitney Ave.

69

15

Armory St.

63

Edgehill Rd.

243

Whalley Ave.

Edwards St.

Goffe

Dixwell

Whitney

York St.

Grove St.

Elm St.

NEW HAVEN

High St.

Green

College St.

START HERE

NORTH

lake, turn right onto Downs Road and skirt Lake Watrous. After the lake, you have a steep uphill ride to Carmel Road, the second road to the right after Lake Watrous, and 2³/₁₀ miles past Downs Road. Turn right onto Carmel Road, down to Brooks Road, where you turn left and proceed for a mile to West Woods Road. Turn right on West Woods. At Choate, West Woods goes right and then loops gently to the left. At Shepard Street, go left for 1 block and then turn right back onto West Woods, which will now take you 1 mile to Whitney Avenue. Turn right onto Whitney, then left onto Mt. Carmel Avenue. On the right you will see the Jonathan Dickerman House, built in 1770. It is open on summer weekends and is worth visiting. On the left is Sleeping Giant State Park. There is a bike rack inside the entrance.

When leaving the park, proceed on Mt. Carmel past Quinnipiac College to Ridge Road; turn right. Ridge Road goes up and down for about 2 miles before leveling off. When you come to a T intersection, turn right, following Ridge Road as it goes up and over Route 22 and then bears gently to the left. Continue on Ridge Road for 3 miles to Waite Street, where you turn right, run downhill to Whitney Avenue and turn left. Here is a stunning view of East Rock across Lake Whitney. You are about 4 miles from your starting point on the New Haven Green.

Follow Whitney Avenue to Armory Street across from the dam. Turn right, then go left on Edgehill Road. (If you're ready for a respite, turn into Edgerton Park on the left.) Follow Edgehill (which soon changes its name to St. Ronan) to Edwards Street, a T intersection. Turn left, go to Whitney once more, and turn right. At Grove Street, turn right, then turn left at College and back to your car.

New Haven — Lighthouse Point

Number of miles:	13
Approximate pedalling time:	2 hours
Terrain:	flat with several small hills
Surface:	good to excellent
Things to see:	New Haven Green, Morris Cove, Lighthouse Point Park, Pardee Morris House, Wooster Square

New Haven—Lighthouse Point was one of our first rides, and it's still a favorite. You'll get to see some interesting parts of New Haven, like the Wooster Square area, take a swim with a picnic (we're great on picnicking) at New Haven's only public beach, and finish with a ride on a beautifully restored carousel. Start at the New Haven Green, on the corner of Church and Elm streets. You can park your car at any spot around the Green. Go east on Elm over the railroad tracks; bear right onto Olive Street. Continue on Olive about ½ mile until you come to Water Street; turn left. Go under the turnpike and over the drawbridge onto what is now Forbes Avenue. After 6 blocks, start up the hill, which spirals right, then left, and peaks at the junction with Woodward Avenue, the first stoplight (it may not be marked). Turn right; cross over I–95 and go straight on Woodward Avenue. After about a mile you'll come to Rayham Road (spelled Raynham at the upper end), the street after the caution light. Stop and take a look. Sitting at the top of the hill, you'll see a large Victorian mansion, just the width of Raynham Road. It's the Townshend mansion, owned and occupied by the same family since 1840. In 1½ miles, Woodward and the water meet at Nathan Hale Park. Woodward Avenue turns inland here and ends as it runs into Townsend Avenue. Turn right and

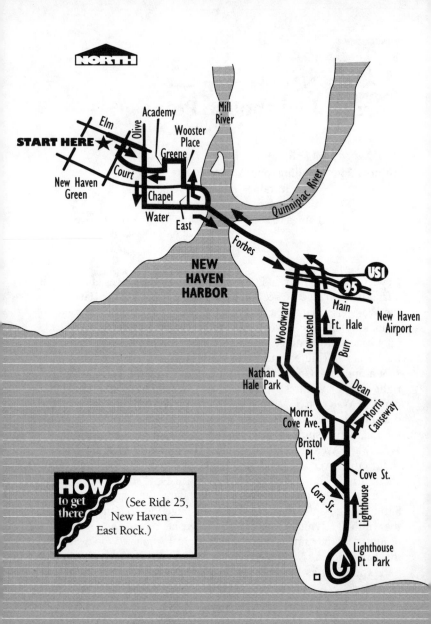

NORTH

Elm
Olive
Academy
Wooster
Place
Greene
START HERE ★
Court
New Haven
Green
Chapel
Water
East
Mill
River

Quinnipiac River

Forbes

NEW
HAVEN
HARBOR

US1
95

Woodward
Townsend
Main
Ft. Hale
Burr

New Haven Airport

Nathan
Hale Park

Dean

Morris
Cove Ave.

Morris
Causeway

Bristol
Pl.

Cove St.

Cora St.

Lighthouse

Lighthouse
Pt. Park

HOW to get there (See Ride 25, New Haven — East Rock.)

within ½ mile, you come to Morris Cove, where you'll have a fine view of New Haven Harbor. Turn right onto Morris Cove Avenue at the end of the cove. Turn left in ½ block when it ends at Bristol Place. Turn right at the intersection with Lighthouse and right again on Cove Street, then left on Cora Street, back to Lighthouse Avenue and the entrance to Lighthouse Point Park. Turn right into the park. It's ½ mile to the beach proper, a lovely beach with a bathhouse and an old-fashioned carousel full of lovingly restored wooden horses. Closed on Mondays only. Lighthouse Point also has the rare distinction of being one of the rest stops for monarch butterflies during their annual migration to central Mexico. During the last week of September and first week of October, the butterflies alight in a tree near the carousel to rest before flying (or is it fluttering?) on to Mexico.

From the park you return to Lighthouse Road, and within ½ mile, you will find the Pardee Morris House on the right, built in 1685 and open to the public from May 1 to Nov. 1 on Saturdays and Sundays only from 11:30 A.M. to 4:00 P.M.

From the Morris House, continue downhill to Townsend Avenue. Cross Townsend onto the very short Morris Causeway to Dean Street; turn left. Continue to Burr Street; turn right and go to Fort Hale Road, the first street on the left past the airport terminal (which has a nifty restaurant overlooking the runways). Turn left and ride uphill to Townsend Avenue where you turn right. Soon you will cross Main Street and I-95. Turn left at the next street, Forbes Avenue. Ride past Woodward, downhill, reversing your outbound track, going over the drawbridge to a right-hand turn at East Street, the first after crossing the bridge. Turn left at the next light, onto Chapel Street. At Wooster Place turn right and make a circuit of Wooster Park, with a left on Greene and a left on Academy. Midway down Academy, turn right onto Court, a short pedestrian/bicycle-only street between Academy and Olive. Continue across Olive, over the railroad, past State and Orange, using the sidewalk since the street is one way in the opposite direction, to Church Street and the New Haven Green.

Old Saybrook

Number of miles:	12
Approximate pedalling time:	1¼ hours
Terrain:	flat
Surface:	good
Things to see:	eighteenth-century houses, Connecticut River, Long Island Sound, Old Saybrook, Fenwick, the Castle Inn at Cornfield Point

This ride takes you on a tour of Old Saybrook's considerable waterfront: North Cove, Saybrook Point, Lynde Point, and Cornfield Point, with stops in between, including a soda or ice cream cone at a soda fountain that's been serving them since 1896! Park at any convenient spot on Main Street and ride south on Main (Route 154). When you reach the large Congregational church at the end of the shopping area, note on your right the old James Pharmacy and Soda Fountain with its large gold mortar and pestle. It was built in 1790 and operated as a pharmacy from 1877 until 1917 by one Peter Lane. In 1917, Lane turned the pharmacy over to his sister-in-law, Ana James, the first black woman pharmacist in Connecticut, who ran it as James Pharmacy until 1967. The soda fountain dates back to 1896—don't pass it by!

At the large arrow traffic sign bear left. (Route 154 is now called College Street.) When you come to North Cove Road, turn left and follow it to the shore of North Cove, a large, protected anchorage, chock-full of sailboats large and small—mostly large—swinging at their moorings. Continue around on Cromwell Place, which leads you back to College Street. Turn left onto College Street and follow it

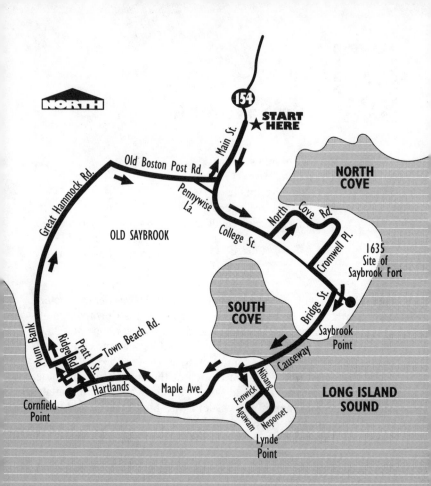

NORTH

154
★ START HERE

NORTH COVE

Main St.

Old Boston Post Rd.

Great Hammock Rd.

Pennywise La.

OLD SAYBROOK

North Cove Rd.

College St.

Cromwell Pl.

1635 Site of Saybrook Fort

SOUTH COVE

Bridge St.

Saybrook Point

Plum Bank

Ridge Rd.

Pratt St.

Town Beach Rd.

Causeway

LONG ISLAND SOUND

Cornfield Point

Hartlands

Maple Ave.

Nibang

Fenwick

Agawam

Neponset

Lynde Point

HOW to get there

From the north, take Route 9 to I–95, go west to Exit 67, and follow Route 154 into Old Saybrook.

From the east, take I–95 to Exit 67, turn left, and go straight to East Main Street.

down to the riverside. There is a new marina as well as an inn on the right and several restaurants on the left. A picnic lunch can be enjoyed on the quay. An even better spot would be the park on the left just before the river, Fort Saybrook Monument Park (which has a public restroom).

When you are ready, return to College Street, turn left on what is now Bridge Street, and cross the causeway over South Cove. This is narrow, so ride carefully. The road is now called Maple Avenue. Turn left on the other side onto Nibang Avenue and take a mile-long circuit of Lynde Point. Back on Maple Avenue, turn left and you will soon find yourself riding beside Long Island Sound.

In the distance, you will see what appears to be a large stone mansion. To get to it, turn left on Hartlands Drive, between two stone pillars. Continue until you get to the Castle Inn, built in 1906 to rival the grandeur of Newport. Here you can get a room, a drink, or a meal.

When you leave the inn, turn left on Pratt Street, left on Town Beach Road, and immediately right on Ridge Road. In 2 blocks, you'll be back on Route 154, now called Plum Bank Road. It continues along the Sound, slowly swings inland, crosses Back River, and becomes Great Hammock Road. About 1½ miles from the inn, Great Hammock Road forms a tee with the Old Boston Post Road. Turn right here and return to Main Street 7/10 mile away.

Mystic—Stonington

Number of miles:	14½
Approximate pedalling time:	2 hours
Terrain:	generally flat, three hills
Surface:	good to only fair in spots; good shoulders where needed
Things to see:	Mystic, Mystic Seaport Museum, Stonington, Old Stone Lighthouse, Mystic Marinelife Aquarium

There are so many things to see on this ride that you just may have to come back and do it again. Start from the south (second) parking lot of Mystic Seaport Museum, just across from its entrance. Mount up and turn left onto Main Street. Turn immediately right on Isham Street. Ride the brief block to the Mystic River and turn left onto Bay Street. When Bay forms a tee with Holmes Street, turn right. At the stop sign, turn left on East Main Street, then turn right at the Civil War Memorial onto Route 1. *Note:* If traffic is backed up in the right lane on Holmes waiting for the drawbridge over on the right, go around the traffic to East Main.

Stonington is 4 miles away. In about 3 miles, St. Mary's Cemetery will be on your right. Make a loop through it and turn right, back onto Route 1. Then turn right again on Route 1A (Water Street) toward Stonington Village.

Turn left on Trumbull Avenue. You will soon come to a stop sign at the foot of the only bridge over the railroad tracks; turn right to go over the bridge, then turn left onto Water Street, and begin the ride down to Stonington Point. The whole town is rich with eighteenth-century buildings, so you'll probably want to explore it thoroughly.

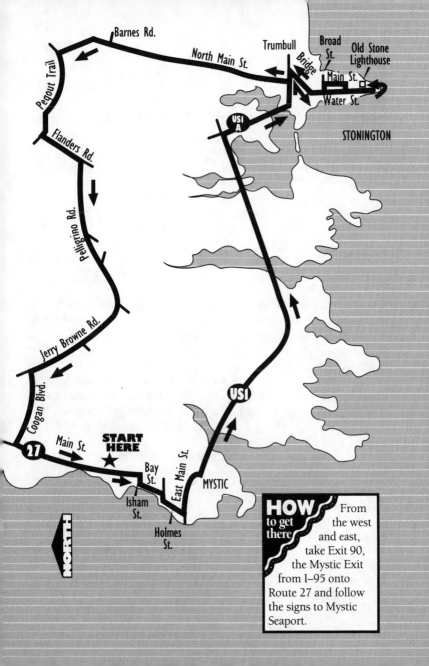

Barnes Rd.

North Main St.

Trumbull

Broad St.

Old Stone Lighthouse

Bridge

Main St.

Water St.

STONINGTON

Pequot Trail

Flanders Rd.

Pelligrino Rd.

USI A

Jerry Browne Rd.

Coogan Blvd.

27

Main St.

START HERE

USI

Bay St.

Isham St.

East Main St.

MYSTIC

Holmes St.

NORTH

HOW to get there From the west and east, take Exit 90, the Mystic Exit from I–95 onto Route 27 and follow the signs to Mystic Seaport.

Just before the end of Water Street, you will see the Old Stone Lighthouse, which is open to the public every day except Monday from 11:00 A.M. to 4:30 P.M., May through October, for a small fee. At this point you are at the halfway point of the ride.

Proceed back up Water Street until you spot the sign that directs all traffic to the right around a tiny park. Turn right and then left onto Main Street. Notice the Old Custom House and the Portuguese Holy Ghost Society, a reminder of the Portuguese fishermen who settled in Stonington and still ply their dangerous calling from her docks. In these days of automated food factories and huge floating factory "fishing" ships, it's good to discover that men still go down to the sea in small boats to bring us fish and clams and oysters. Turn left on Broad Street and then right on Water Street to go back over the bridge. On the other side of the bridge, take an immediate left onto Trumbull and then a right onto North Main Street, which quickly becomes a country road. Then 2½ miles after your turn onto North Main Street, you'll come to a T intersection with Pequot Trail; turn left. After you see the "Road Church" on your left and just before the road goes over the turnpike, turn left onto Flanders Road (it may not be marked). In ³⁄₁₀ mile, turn right onto Pelligrino Road and go uphill. Continue on Pelligrino when Montauk Avenue comes in from the left. After the stop sign, just past Deans Mill Road, continue straight. Pelligrino Road becomes Jerry Browne Road at the point where Mistuxet comes in from the left. Continue on Jerry Browne Road uphill and down. Turn left onto Coogan Boulevard just before going under the turnpike. Coogan goes past the Mystic Marinelife Aquarium and the Old Mystic Village Shopping Center. Coogan makes a tee at Route 27 at a busy intersection in a snarl of motels and gas stations. Turn left and head back to Mystic Seaport.

North Lyme

Number of miles:	12½
Approximate pedalling time:	1½ hours
Terrain:	definitely hilly
Surface:	fair
Things to see:	lovely country throughout, Eight Mile River, Hamburg, North Lyme

This has always been one of the most popular rides because of the beautiful countryside and the thrilling downhill runs. The best place to park your vehicle is on the side road off Route 156 that is to the right just before the large sign, NEHANTIC STATE FOREST, 800 FEET.

Mount up and turn right onto Route 156. Proceed uphill; at the crest you will enjoy a scene of rolling hills and pastures. After a whopping downhill, a brief uphill will deliver you to the town of Hamburg, which borders the Eight Mile River. Soon after you pass a Congregational church, the road forks; take the left fork, Old Hamburg Road, down to the river's edge. When the road comes to a tee, turn right. After turning you'll notice a good place to picnic at the riverside on your left.

When you return to Route 156, turn left. The road follows the Eight Mile River for a time, meandering and going up and down. Just after you cross Beaver Brook, turn right onto Beaver Brook Road. For nearly 3 miles go along this two-lane country road, passing farms and handsome country houses. You will pass a road coming in from the right and then arrive at the intersection of Beaver Brook, Gungy (on the left), and Grassy Hill roads. Turn right onto Grassy Hill Road. You pass through a beautiful forest here whose dappled light makes this a perfect ride for a summer evening. When you come out of the woods,

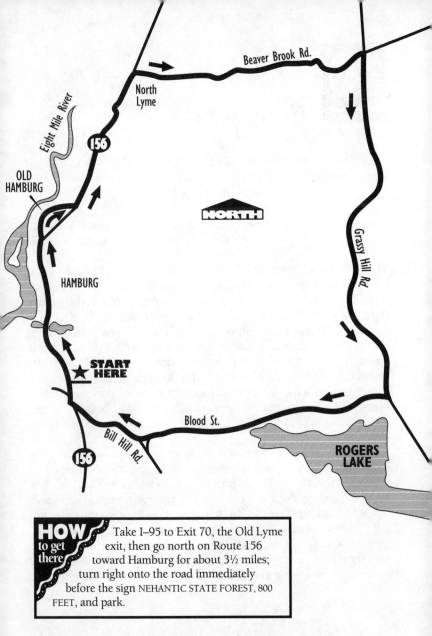

Beaver Brook Rd.

North
Lyme

Eight Mile River

156

OLD
HAMBURG

NORTH

Grassy Hill Rd.

HAMBURG

**START
HERE**

Blood St.

Bill Hill Rd.

156

**ROGERS
LAKE**

HOW
to get
there

Take I–95 to Exit 70, the Old Lyme
exit, then go north on Route 156
toward Hamburg for about 3½ miles;
turn right onto the road immediately
before the sign NEHANTIC STATE FOREST, 800
FEET, and park.

the hill crests yielding a spacious view and a surprising field of ferns on the right. The Congregational church is set high on the hill to your left. A settled area follows this scene, and there are some steep downhills to the point where you turn off Grassy Hill Road.

A landmark for the turn right onto Blood Street is an abandoned windmill; it is not the Dutch type, but has a metal superstructure topped by narrow blades. There may not be a sign for Blood Street, so keep an eye out for the windmill. Blood Street borders Rogers Lake. This stretch is a rather densely populated resort area where there are a couple of steep hills. In about $1\frac{1}{2}$ miles bear right at the fork and go right again when the road forms a tee with Bill Hill Road, just a few feet from the fork. Continue to the right as Bill Hill Road returns you to Route 156. Turn right when you reach 156, and in $\frac{1}{5}$ mile you will be back at your starting place.

Waterford—New London

Number of miles:	13¾
Approximate pedalling time:	1¾ hours
Terrain:	mostly flat, a couple of steep hills
Surface:	only fair in Waterford, good in New London
Things to see:	Atlantic Ocean, Thames River and New London Harbor, Harkness Memorial State Park, Ocean Beach Park

This circuit of Waterford and the western shore of New London Harbor will show you many things and give you a choice of many things to do in only 13¾ miles. The best place to start from is the town hall parking lot on the right side of Route 156, just west of the junction of Routes 1 and 156 in Waterford. (The renovated Town Hall has nice restrooms.)

Proceed west on 156 about ½ mile to Great Neck Road (Route 213), where you turn left. Great Neck narrows, so use the sidewalk on this stretch. Just before Great Neck swings to the left, down toward the Harkness Estate, you'll catch a stunning glimpse of the ocean. About 3½ miles into the ride, you reach the entrance to Harkness Memorial State Park. We recommend you stop here to visit the Newport-style mansion, with its enormous lawns and beautiful gardens.

Return to Route 213 and turn right, following signs to New London. At the first stop sign, turn right. At the next stop sign, turn left. (The O'Neill Theater is on the right.) Turn right when the road makes a tee at Niles Hill Road. Go up Niles Hill. At the traffic light turn right onto Ocean Avenue, a T intersection, following the signs to Ocean

START HERE

Post Rd.

Clark La.

US1

Willetts Ave.

156

NORTH

Ocean Ave.

Orient Pt. Ferry

School St.

Pequot Ave.

Great Neck Rd.

Niles Hill Rd.

ALEWIFE COVE

Ocean Ave.

Pequot Ave.

213

Eugene O'Neill Memorial Theater

Neptune Ave.

Great Neck Rd.

GOSHEN COVE

Harkness Memorial State Park

Ocean Beach

Goshen Point

HOW to get there — From the east or west, take I–95 to Exit 75, then go east on Route 1 (Boston Post Road) 4.8 miles, past three traffic lights to the fourth light at the junction of Route 1 and Route 156 west; turn right onto Route 156 and turn into the parking lot of the town hall.

Beach Park. Ocean Avenue is broad but very busy in the summer. When you reach Neptune Avenue, turn right and ride to the entrance to Ocean Beach Park. The park has a wide beach, well-maintained boardwalk, rides, restaurants, arcade, miniature golf, and water slide; this is a marvelous place to linger over lunch!

Return to Neptune Avenue, cross Ocean Avenue, and turn left onto Pequot Avenue. (Pequot is Mott Avenue to the right of Neptune.) You will enjoy an unobstructed view of New London's outer harbor as you ride along Pequot. As you approach downtown New London, you'll enter an area featuring small marinas and restaurants. Also Monte Cristo Cottage, the boyhood home of Eugene O'Neill, now a museum at 325 Pequot Avenue, about six houses before Thames Street. It's open Monday through Friday from 1:00 to 4:00 P.M.

At School Street, turn left and climb back up to Ocean Avenue; turn right. In less than a mile, you'll come to Willetts Avenue. Turn left up a gentle incline, then downhill to Route 1, where there is a traffic light. Make your left-hand turn carefully onto this busy highway. At Clark Lane and the next traffic light, be alert again. Go straight ahead, getting into the left lane so that you can turn forty-five degrees to the left onto Route 156 west, and return to the parking lot just beyond the intersection.

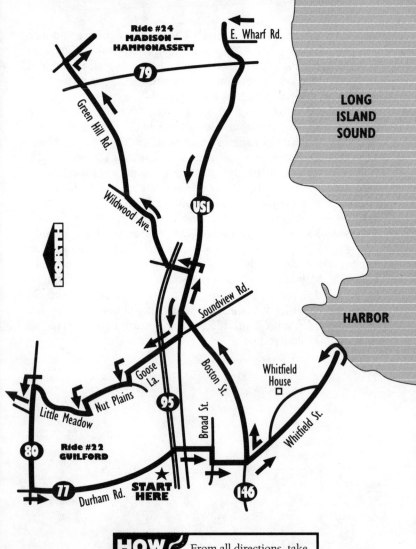

Ride #24
**MADISON —
HAMMONASSETT**

E. Wharf Rd.

79

Green Hill Rd.

Wildwood Ave.

USI

NORTH

**LONG
ISLAND
SOUND**

Soundview Rd.

HARBOR

Goose La.

Boston St.

Whitfield
House

95

Nut Plains

Little Meadow

Broad St.

Whitfield St.

80

Ride #22
GUILFORD

77 Durham Rd. **START
HERE**

146

HOW
to get
there
From all directions, take
I–95 to Exit 58, and
proceed to the commuter
parking lots on Route 77, on the
north side of 95.

Combination:
Guilford & Madison—Hammonasset

Number of miles:	38
Approximate pedalling time:	4 hours
Terrain:	mostly flat; a couple of steep hills, and two long downhills
Surface:	good
Things to see:	Guilford Green and harbor, Henry Whitfield House, Hammonasset State Park

Here you have an opportunity to combine race training (if such is your pleasure) and sight-seeing. There are a couple of hills that offer a challenge, some fascinating sights along the way, and 2 miles of sand and sun at Hammonasset—all in 38 miles of bicycling—the way to go.

Start at the commuter parking lot on Route 77, just north of I–95 in Guilford, where you can leave your car or what-have-you. Follow the directions in Ride No. 22, Guilford, down 77 to the harbor.

When you return up Whitfield Drive, turn right on Boston Street. When you reach Soundview Road, don't turn left; continue straight for the short distance to the T with Route 1, where you bear right and continue on Ride No. 24, Madison—Hammonasset (see page 93).

When you get to the end of this 17-mile ride, at Goose Lane on the north side of I–95, continue straight up Goose Lane and do the second half of the Guilford ride. This will take you on a jaunt through the North Guilford countryside, past Route 80 and then back down 77 to your starting place. This 38-mile circuit gives you a nice workout and the reward of a 4-mile downhill at the end.

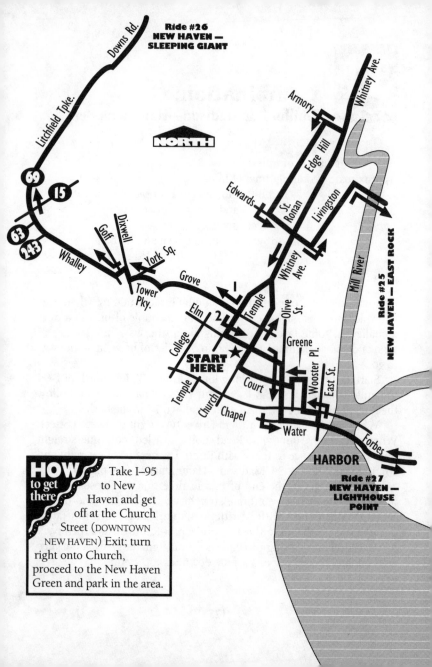

Combination:
New Haven—East Rock, Lighthouse Point, and Sleeping Giant

Number of miles:	47
Approximate pedalling time:	5 hours
Terrain:	flat in the city, a steep hill to East Rock summit, a long hill in the first half of the ride to Sleeping Giant
Surface:	good
Things to see:	New Haven, East Rock and its view, Wooster Square, Lighthouse Park, Sleeping Giant State Park

This combination makes a good race-training ride, with its 47 miles of varied terrain, flat city streets with traffic to contend with, steep sprint to the summit of East Rock, and long endurance uphill through the countryside.

The ride has the shape of a three-leaf clover: the stem is rooted in the New Haven Green, with the first leaf curving out to the north to East Rock Park and back: the second leaf reaches out to the northwest, then east to Sleeping Giant State Park, and back to the Green in New Haven; and the third leaf stretches east to the beach at Lighthouse Point and back through Wooster Square.

Start from the Green and head north on Church Street, following the directions in Ride No. 25, New Haven—East Rock, for the 9 miles to the Rock and back. Next, take off for Sleeping Giant from College Street to High to Grove and over to Whalley, following the instructions in ride No. 26, New Haven—Sleeping Giant.

When you return to the center of town after this 25-mile stretch, you might be ready for a swim, so, head down Elm Street, following the New Haven—Lighthouse Point route (Ride No. 27) to the beach by the New Haven harbor breakwater. When you are completely refreshed, follow the map and directions back to the starting point.

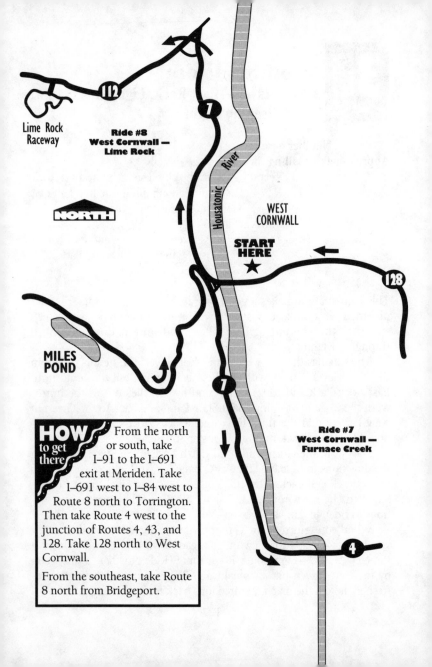

Lime Rock Raceway

Ride #8
West Cornwall —
Lime Rock

112

7

Housatonic River

NORTH

WEST CORNWALL

START HERE ★

128

MILES POND

7

Ride #7
West Cornwall —
Furnace Creek

HOW to get there
From the north or south, take I–91 to the I–691 exit at Meriden. Take I–691 west to I–84 west to Route 8 north to Torrington. Then take Route 4 west to the junction of Routes 4, 43, and 128. Take 128 north to West Cornwall.

From the southeast, take Route 8 north from Bridgeport.

4

34 Combination:
West Cornwall—Furnace Creek & West Cornwall—Lime Rock

Number of miles:	26
Approximate pedalling time:	3½ hours
Terrain:	definitely hilly but with several fine downhills
Surface:	good
Things to see:	an 1837 covered bridge (see and use), the hillside village of West Cornwall, Housatonic River, Furnace Creek, Lime Rock Raceway, the Wildlife Sanctuary, the splendor of northwest Connecticut's mountains and forests

Since both rides start from West Cornwall, you can begin with either one. I would suggest doing Ride No. 8, Lime Rock, first, for then you can continue with No. 7, Furnace Creek, without going through West Cornwall.

The best place to park is in the small Post Office lot on the right side of the street facing the river. When you are ready to ride, go over the river through the one-lane covered bridge and turn right if you choose to do Lime Rock first, or left if you have opted for Furnace Creek first. Both rides end with a fine and fitting downhill.

Follow the directions in the book for each ride, and when you're back in West Cornwall you can relax at that fine little restaurant that overlooks the creek.

About the Author

Edwin Mullen is a "Clamdigger." He qualified for that title by being born in May of 1924 on City Island, a tiny island that sits just off the coast of the Bronx borough of New York City. Drafted into the Army at age 18, he survived a brief stint as a twin-engine bomber pilot, dropping explosive devices on hapless German soldiers in Italy, which taught him that war was not the grand and glorious adventure he had been led to expect it to be.

He has been an actor, producer, purchasing agent for Yale University, and now, contentedly retired from the latter, a freelance writer and actor, working for himself and his readers.

Other books of interest from The Globe Pequot Press:

Short Bike Rides series

Short Bike Rides in Rhode Island, Third Edition

Short Bike Rides in Greater Boston and
Central Massachusetts, Third Edition

Short Bike Rides on Long Island, Third Edition

Short Bike Rides on Cape Cod, Nantucket
and the Vineyard, Fourth Edition

Short Bike Rides in New Jersey, Second Edition

Short Bike Rides in and around New York City

Short Nature Walks series

Short Nature Walks on Cape Cod and The Vineyard, Third Edition

Sixty Selected Short Nature Walks in Connecticut, Third Edition

Short Nature Walks on Long Island, Third Edition

Best Bike Rides in New England

Recommended Country Inns New England, Twelfth Edition

Bed & Breakfast in New England, Third Edition

Daytrips, Getaway Weekends, and Vacations in
New England, Third Edition

Guide to Nantucket, Fifth Edition

Guide to Martha's Vineyard, Fifth Edition

Guide to Cape Cod

In and Out of Boston With (or Without) Children, Fourth Edition

Boston's Freedom Trail

For a free catalogue of Globe Pequot's quality books on travel, nature,
gardening, cooking, crafts, recreation, and more, please write
The Globe Pequot Press, Box Q, Chester, Connecticut 06412,
or call toll-free 1–800–243–0495 or
1–800–962–0973 (in Connecticut)
to place your order.